ANXIETY WORKBOOK

"Which Guides You to Get Out of the Hole"

"There is only one way to happiness and that is to cease worrying about things which are beyond the power of our will."
—Epictetus

Mary Curry

TABLE OF CONTENTS

INTRODUCTION

Dear Readers,

Welcome to the Anxiety Workbook which guides you to get you out of the hole. Probably if you have been given this book it is because you have some experience with anxiety in your life and you are looking for ways to either rid yourself of it or to learn how to cope with it.

Anxiety is normal, and you're not abnormal. Everyone experiences anxiety at least once in their lives. There are many ways to treat anxiety. This book contains many activities, which can be used to reduce anxiety and prevent it from occurring in the first place. It may seem strange at first that some of these activities are taking place. There may be times when you are asked to do something totally new.

Also, you may find that some activities help you while others do not. It's normal, too. As a unique individual, you'll have to find the activities that work best for you.

Keep taking steps towards peace as you practice patience with yourself. Although it may take you some time to find the answers, be assured they are there! Keeping to the path will help you find them.

Thanks!

ANXIETY

During times of stress, your body responds naturally with anxiety. You feel this way because you're anxious about what's to come. Most people feel nervous and fearful on the first day of school, in an interview, or while giving a speech.

You may have anxiety disorder if your feelings of anxiety are extreme, last for a long period of time, and/or interfere with your daily life.

Each person experiences anxiety differently. You might feel butterflies in your stomach, or your heart may race. Feeling out of control can make you feel disconnected from your body.

Anxiety can also manifest as nightmares, panic attacks, or painful thoughts or memories that you cannot control. You may feel scared and worried in general, or you may fear a particular place or event.

Anxiety symptoms include:

- Increasing heart rate
- Breathing rapidly
- Restlessness
- Concentration difficulties
- Having trouble falling asleep

Someone else may experience totally different anxiety symptoms than you do. Because of this, it's crucial to know how anxiety manifests itself.

CHEMISTRY OF ANXIETY

When you start a new job, move to a new place, or take a test, it's normal to feel anxious. You may find that this type of anxiety motivates you to work harder and to do a better job, but it is unpleasant. Anxiety can interfere with your daily life, but it is not a persistent feeling.

Anxiety disorders may cause a feeling of constant fear. The pain can be debilitating and intense.

Anxiety like this can prevent you from doing the things you enjoy. You may not be able to enter an elevator, cross the street, or even leave your home in the worst case scenario. Anxiety grows worse if not treated.

Among all types of emotional disorders, anxiety disorders are the most common. Anxiety disorders are more likely to affect women than men, according to the American Psychiatric Association.

When you feel apprehension, worry, distress, or fear, you are said to be having an anxiety attack. Often, anxiety attacks develop slowly. When a stressful event approaches, it may worsen.

Individuals may experience different anxiety attacks and experience different symptoms. Because anxiety is a condition that comes in many forms, and not all of its symptoms occur at the same time.

A panic attack may present with symptoms such as:

- Faintness or dizziness
- Breathlessness
- Mouth feeling dry
- Sweating
- Hot flashes or chills
- Worry
- Restlessness
- Embarrassment
- Afraid
- Tingling or numbness

Mary Curry

Peace Is Already Within You

"Never be in a hurry; do everything quietly and in a calm spirit. Do not lose your inner peace for anything whatsoever, even if your whole world seems upset." – Saint Francis de Sales

The question is: Where is the peace—for our nations, our families, and above all for our souls? Since ancient times, people have cried out in this way. Do you also feel this way?

Almost everyone is weary and stressed. There is no doubt that a person needs direction and advice, security and confidence. A peaceful mind is something we all need and desire.

The treasure of peace of mind! In a world so full of conflict, despair and turmoil, where are you going to find this treasure?

It's time for the great hunt! Often, people seek peace through love and relationships, fame and fortune, power and pleasure. Despite their attempts at filling their minds and wallets with knowledge, their souls remain empty. Those who abuse drugs and alcohol seek escape from life's realities, but their goal isn't achieved. Their minds and bodies are still troubled, and they are still empty and lonely.

Most people believe that we find or achieve peace only by working hard within ourselves. The state of peace is already within us, but it remains hidden under all of the stress we experience in our day-to-day lives.

Whenever you have stressful thoughts or think about covering up your peace, you are in fact doing so. If you keep dwelling on the anxiety, you may forget your peace. Thoughts don't destroy peace, but they can disrupt it and make it difficult to remember.

SELF AFFIRMATION

Affirmations are specific types of positive statements that are normally directed at yourself in order to promote change and self-love while squashing worry and fear.

Affirmations are a form of positive self-talk that can alter your subconscious thoughts.

It gives an encouraging or supportive phrase more power to be repeated, because hearing something repeatedly increases your likelihood of believing it. As a result, your belief influences your behavior in a way that makes your affirmation a reality.

Affirmations can strengthen self-worth by increasing your positive opinion of yourself and your confidence in your ability to achieve your goals. Medications can also alleviate symptoms of anxiety such as panic and stress.

You can start changing your thought patterns when your anxious thoughts overwhelm you and make it difficult to concentrate on more positive possibilities.

WHAT AFFIRMATIONS CAN AND CAN'T DO

In addition to creating and reinforcing new attitudes and behaviors, affirmations can't solve your anxiety problems magically.

Here are some things they _can_ do:

- Boost your mood
- Enhance self-esteem
- Boost motivation
- Solve your problems
- Positive outlook boosts optimism

- Negative thoughts can be addressed with affirmations

Affirmations that hold a basis in reality tend to have a much greater impact when dealing with anxiety. Trying to convince yourself that you can do things that aren't realistic might make you doubt yourself and make you return to feeling incompetent and unsuccessful.

Imagine you are concerned about your financial situation *a lot*.

The best you can do is repeat "I'll win the lottery" every day, no matter how unrealistically positive this is. In contrast, affirmations such as "I am talented and experienced enough to find a higher paying job" may provide you with motivation to accomplish this.

As affirmation activates the reward system in the brain, it may work in part to reducing pain perception, this system can also soften the impact of physical pain and emotional stress.

As a result, affirming yourself improves your ability to handle challenges.

It is often easier to work toward lasting change when you are confident that you can manage any situation.

CREATING YOUR OWN AFFIRMATIONS

You have probably seen plenty of lists of affirmations, along with suggestions to "choose affirmations that resonate with you." If you have started exploring affirmations already, you are likely to have found many lists.

Although that's a good idea, creating your own affirmations feels even more natural and right.

"I am fearless," is a common affirmation.

The phrase "I have anxious thoughts but I can challenge and change them" might be more believable and useful if you rewrite it, perhaps as: "I have anxious thoughts *and* I can challenge and change them."

Are you ready to begin? Remember these tips.

BEGIN WITH "I" OR "MY"

First-person perspectives can strengthen the connection between affirmations and your sense of self. Their relevance to specific goals makes them more credible, so their credibility is enhanced.

KEEP THEM IN THE PRESENT TENSE

My goal for next year is to seem more confident in conversations with people.

However, affirmations aren't necessarily goals. By rewriting your existing thought patterns, you can improve your self-esteem and reduce anxiety. As you set them for a future date, you tell yourself, "Sure, that will happen eventually."

You may not notice much of a difference in the way you behave today, however, structure your affirmation with a sense that it *is* already true. If you believe it is true and act accordingly, the likelihood of it becoming true increases.

For example; I am confident about talking to strangers and making new friends.

Don't Be Afraid to Accept Anxious Thoughts

Affirmations may prove helpful for people who experience anxiety. In addition, affirmations can become more powerful if they are based on reality.

You should use positive words and focus on what you would like to achieve.

The alternative is: "I will not let my anxiety affect my work anymore."

Try saying: "Despite my worries about failure, I *can* accomplish my goals."

Tie Them to Core Values and Successes

You're reminded of your core values when you connect your affirmations to them.

Repetition of these affirmations reinforces self-confidence and cultivates greater self-empowerment.

Affirming compassion can help you keep in mind that self-compassion is equally important:

"I treat myself with the same kindness as I show my family and friends."

You can also use affirmations to defeat self-defeating thoughts by remembering your previous accomplishments:

"I feel stressed, but I know it will pass. Due to my past experience, I can cope with panic and calm myself down."

HOW TO USE THEM

Let's say you already know a few affirmations for starting; how do you use them?

Although there is no "right" or "wrong" answer, these tips can help you maximize your time.

CREATE A DAILY ROUTINE

When you repeat affirmations during stressful times, it can be helpful, but it usually has the best results when you practice them on a regular basis rather than just when you need it most.

They are no different from any other habit. Regular practice is essential to seeing lasting changes, isn't it?

You should commit to affirming yourself for 30 days at a time. Keep in mind that results may not be as immediate as they seem.

Spend a few minutes repeating your affirmations two or three times a day. The use of affirmations at the beginning of the day and at night is helpful for many people.

Maintain a consistent schedule, regardless of the time you choose. If 10 is your lucky number, make sure you repeat each affirmation 10 times.

A mirror can be an effective tool for affirmations that promote the belief that "Seeing is believing." Do not just rattle them off, think about them and believe they are true!

Affirmations can even be incorporated into your daily meditation practice or may be visualized to make them more real to you.

Keep Them Current

You can always revise and restructure your affirmations to make them more effective.

Be aware of your progress over time. What has been the impact of the affirmations on your ability to control your worries and to practice self-compassion when you feel down? Because you don't believe them yet, do they not have much impact?

You can use these successes as inspiration and even devise new affirmations when you see them working.

Keep Them Where You Can See them

It is helpful to see your affirmations frequently so that they stay at the forefront of your mind.

Try:

- You can leave sticky notes or memos on your desk and around the house
- Adding them to your phone's notification list
- Affirmations should be written at the start of every journal entry

Reaching Out

When anxiety becomes severe enough, it can affect all aspects of a person's life, including:

- Partnerships
- Health and fitness
- Work and school performance
- Responsibilities on a daily basis

While affirmations can be effective as self-help strategies, they might not be enough to relieve severe or persistent anxiety symptoms.

Speak to a doctor about your symptoms if anxiety is negatively affecting your daily life. A medical issue can sometimes cause symptoms.

When dealing with anxiety symptoms, many people need a therapist's support, and that's OK. You shouldn't feel bad about your affirmations.

A therapist can help you uncover the underlying causes of anxiety, which cannot be accomplished with affirmations. You can deal with anxiety symptoms more effectively if you learn what triggers them.

Get started on your journey to affordable therapy with our guide.

THE BOTTOM LINE

Despite their power, affirmations may not be effective for everyone - though many people find them helpful.

This doesn't mean you've done anything wrong if affirmations don't provide any results or decrease your distress. The fact that you may need another type of support just means you might be able to benefit from something else.

Positive self-talk can boost your self-esteem over time, but it isn't a cure-all. If you don't seem to be progressing, it may be more helpful for you to see a therapist.

How to Stop Spiraling Negative Thoughts from Taking Control?

- Remove "should" thoughts
- Recognize automatic negative thinking
- Putting your thoughts on trial
- Acknowledge how overwhelmed you feel
- Don't force positive thoughts

One Gradual Habit Can Become a Powerful Mental Tool

A majority of external wounds can be treated fairly easily. A bandage can be used to heal a cut finger, and antibacterial cream can be applied to close the wound. You're pretty much good to go at this point.

The treatment of your thought processes isn't as straightforward or prescriptive as you might think. Especially if they are caused by mental health conditions like anxiety, depression, or panic attacks.

It's like getting a paper cut over and over again, and no matter what you do, you can't seem to stop. You may not even notice that you have a cut until it starts to sting.

Medications, psychotherapy, and lifestyle approaches for each individual depend on their condition and trigger changes. It is difficult to receive fast treatment when there is no therapy within reach.

One Gradual Habit That Might Help Is Making Mental Shifts

The act of changing your thoughts is the result of consciously stopping a long-held pattern of thought. In order to pay attention to something else, you have to re-evaluate how you think about a particular situation.

Your train of thought won't just loop and re-loop as you switch gears in your brain.

There are a lot of things you need to undo, including negative behavioral patterns and mental programming. If, as a child, you were taught that you had to always do your best in school and in life, you've likely been programmed for chronic perfectionist behavior.

Making a mental shift is a way to combat your anxiety and stress, or snap out of winding thoughts.

Take some time to learn common thought patterns, how to spot automatic negative thinking, and how to provide yourself constructive consideration when you are reorientated.

Whenever you think of "should", stop and think about it

Doing, acting, or feeling better is what I ought to do.

- "I should exercise every day."
- "I should eat more healthy."
- "I shouldn't think like this."

This is not to say that the thoughts behind them are bad. It may be healthier for you to eat whole foods and work out depending on your situation. A word like "should" can harm you. It triggers feelings of guilt that can lead to a downward spiral of negative feelings.

STOP LEADING YOUR THOUGHTS WITH "I SHOULD"

Anxious thought patterns can be caused by statements that place demands on you that are sometimes difficult to meet.

EVERYONE MAKES MISTAKES.

Instead of...	Try...
Every day I should go to the gym.	It will be my goal to exercise every day. Here's how to do it...
It's time to eat healthier.	These things can help me eat healthier today...
The way I think should change.	My thoughts are filled with anxiety right now. How about this one? To my best friend, what would I say?
Anxiety shouldn't stop me from flying.	However, I accept that I have to work towards a solution despite my fear of flying. How can I help in this situation?

There are times when the idea of doing, acting, or feeling something a certain way can be just enough pressure to make you procrastinate or avoid the responsibility or activity entirely. Some people just experience more anxiety because of this.

You should listen to your own thoughts. Would you tell yourself that you should do something? A kinder way to stay motivated would be to think of positive ways to prevent spiraling downwards?

It's important to remember that there are no right ways to do things. We all make mistakes as we grow.

TRY RECOGNIZING OTHER PATTERNS OF AUTOMATIC NEGATIVE THINKING

Automatic negative thoughts (ANTs) could be responsible for these "shoulds." ANTs are a form of cognitive distortion.

An ANT is a reaction that occurs when you feel strongly about something, rather than a rational thought.

Anxiety and depression are prone to this type of thinking.

People with anxiety often turn these thdoughts into panic attacks. ANTs make these the showrunner of their minds.

Despite this, it is not easy to identify ANTs. It could be that you've had them since you were a child.

IDENTIFY AND TACKLE YOUR ANTS BY KEEPING A THOUGHT RECORD

In "Mind Over Mood," a hands-on cognitive behavioral therapy (CBT) workbook, you can do this by breaking a scenario down into three parts:

- Currently, there is a situation
- What's on your mind
- Identifying these thoughts requires that you actively alter them into more helpful, productive, or wise ones.

WHAT SITUATION IS CAUSING YOUR ANXIETY?

You are essentially putting your thoughts to the test when you create a thought record. Consider who, what, where, when, and why. It will allow you to focus on the facts and not your emotions when you describe what happened.

- Did you go with anyone?
- How did you spend your time?
- What did you do?
- What was the date?

WHAT'S YOUR MOOD IN THIS SITUATION?

Then, rate your moods based on a scale of 100 on the intensity of these feelings. An example of your moods when submitting a work project is:

- Frustrated
- Afraid
- Maybe there's guilt if it's late

When anxiety is your dominant mood, you would rate it at 80 percent if nervousness and anxiety are the dominant moods. There would then be 20 percent of irritation and guilt remaining.

Don't stress over the percentage - just go with what feels right to you. When you rate someone, you're mainly noticing how much of what you think is reflected in their ratings - for instance, anxious versus guilt-ridden.

WHAT ARE THE AUTOMATIC THOUGHTS RUNNING THROUGH YOUR MIND?

Your thought record must consist of the following steps: List the images and thoughts that pop into your head related to that situation. Try to recall your thoughts at the time.

There are several automatic thoughts that can occur:

- I'm so stupid.
- This will be a disaster for me.
- No one likes me.
- The world is a terrible place.
- I can't handle this.
- It's likely that I'll be left alone.

A possible solution, if you find yourself caught up in ANTs like these, is to break the situation down into "tasks", as it might help you shift away from your default mindset.

Rather than assuming you will mess up the situation, analyze why you are feeling that way before you begin.

In a work situation, ask yourself if projects have gone awry in the past and you're afraid? What is the difference between this project and those in the past?

Determine how you feel when you consider the worst-case scenario. See if there is any basis for your anxiety or automated thoughts by breaking down your emotions and moods.

Your past and future are unlikely to affect this work situation as you dig deeper into it.

Gaining control over your emotions begins with identifying your automatic thoughts. What do you tell yourself? Do you know how you can change this now?

How Can You Change Your Negative Thinking?

You must put your automatic thoughts to the test once you discover them.

Is this thought supported by evidence? When evidence is derived from the past, why does it apply to a new experience?

Instead of focusing on emotions or thoughts, you should consider credible evidence. Next, you need to examine the evidence that does not support your position.

Here's an example to show you how it works.

I thought to myself: I may mess this up.

According to these credible sources, my perspective is supported:

- Due to a mistake I made, we had to delay the project by a few weeks.
- As a presenter, I have few skills.
- It is the biggest project I have ever undertaken alone.

Against my thought, there is credible evidence

- I discussed timelines with my manager and we came to an agreement.
- Over the past two weeks, I have practiced my presentation in front of a coworker, who gave me helpful feedback.
- Any questions on the topic can be answered by me, since I'm knowledgeable.

Your original idea needs to be reconsidered now

Now that you've heard both sides' argument, it's time to be a judge.

You can help yourself by acting as if you are judging a friend's thoughts rather than your own.

A more balanced thought is now available to you. With this new strategy, your wiser mind will examine all evidence in your favor and against you.

As an example:

- Although I sometimes make mistakes, in general I put a lot of effort into my work."
- "I'm doing my best."
- My manager trusts me to carry out this task. I've received good feedback thus far."

Reminder: Breaking everything down into manageable chunks is possible. You may be able to give yourself a break by taking a moment to pause and check in with yourself.

Understand that emotional roller coasters and burdens are part of life

As with identifying ANTs, acknowledging your feelings of overwhelmingness is also powerful. It's important not to let your anxiety spiral out of control by automatically putting yourself in defensive mode. To combat mental strain, you must welcome it, regardless of whether it is due to stress, anxiety, or another condition.

Why would I ever want to experience all these jitters and shakes?

It takes less energy to embrace it than to dread it.

If you feel this reaction, realize that you're experiencing something that is important to you, rather than using extra energy to fight back. In addition, you may not always have to give your best effort. It's exhausting.

The first step to managing stress is to understand your anxiety and what it means. It's possible that a trigger exists. Eventually, you may stop dreading it or you can take action to avoid it.

Take the time to ask yourself, "Hello, anxiety, what are we going to do today to function together?" Through the stressful event, you may find yourself less inclined to fight against yourself.

Reminder: Even if you opt out or say no, there is always another option. Consider whether you can avoid a particular situation causing you anxiety or stress.

There's a good chance you can!

CHALLENGE YOURSELF TO MAKE SMALL STEPS INSTEAD OF FORCING POSITIVE THOUGHTS

The key to mental shifts is not changing "I feel sad" to "I feel happy."

As a result, general anxiety could be treated much easier and would cease to exist.

Even though you try, you won't be able to change your thought pattern all the time. At times like these, it's important to remember it's enough to merely recognize, or acknowledge, the thought.

It's OK to be sad. It's okay to feel anxious. Taking a break will make you feel better.

You can start by slowly identifying problems and thinking about workarounds when you have the energy to do so.

You'll gain strength and a stronger perspective the more you remind yourself of these things.

Remember, asking for professional help is OK. When you suffer from depression, anxiety or another mental health condition, forcing positive thoughts isn't helpful or authentic. Talk to a mental health care professional if you find that you can't shift your thoughts.

USE THIS 5-MINUTE THERAPY TECHNIQUE EVERY DAY FOR MY ANXIET

The products we include are those we believe are useful for our readers.

Here's our process.

The first thing you must do is identify what kind of cognitive distortion is taking place.

- From the time I can remember, I've struggled with general anxiety. I struggle the most with social and performance anxiety, as I conduct interviews during the day and interact with editors at night, and I also perform stand-up comedy.
- My anxiety is most often manifested in what I call 'anxiety hangovers,' when I wake up feeling terrible about everything I did or said the night before, regardless of how fun and successful the event was.
- I wake up in the morning and am spit on by my inner voice from everyone thinking you're egotistical and obnoxious.
- Because you never think before you speak, you said the exact wrong thing when your friend asked for your opinion.
- You dominated the conversation at dinner. That's why you are unpopular.
- Your performance on stage was so embarrassing. Of course you weren't a success.
- It keeps going and going and going.
- I sometimes experience panic attacks the morning following big events, such as a friend's wedding or a comedy show. Occasionally, I feel mentally paralyzed because of worry and lack the confidence to do my work.

Cognitive Behavioral Therapy Comes In

When you change the way you think, you will change the way you feel. Cognitive Behavioral Therapy (CBT) is based on this simple premise.

Nevertheless, if it were that easy to feel better and escape anxiety and depression, we would not live in a country where psychological distress is on the rise.

My anxiety has not completely disappeared or been cured (and probably never will), but I have discovered a five-minute CBT exercise each day that eases it a bit. Suddenly, my racing thoughts cease, my foggy brain clears, and I feel less fatigued.

Suddenly, I feel ready to face the day.

Dr. David D. Burns' triple column technique, which completely changes mindset. We are not able to completely shut our anxiety down for the day by simply making this shift. Our perspective of ourselves needs to change for us to be able to be calmer, and happier.

RECOGNIZING COGNITIVE DISTORTIONS

First, We had to learn what cognitive distortions were - those statements that We made about who we are and what we were going through.

There are 10 big distortions that can occur:

1. Thinking all or nothing.

Instead of seeing gray in shades of black and white. For instance: I'm not a good person.

2. Overgeneralization.

When you extend a negative thought so it reaches even further. Example: I never do anything right.

3. The mental filter.

Focusing only on the bad stuff after filtering out everything else. The day wasn't productive for me.

4. Disqualifying Positively.

If you believe that a positive or good experience does not contribute to your larger pattern of failure or negativity. As the saying goes, if a clock is wrong once, it is right twice.

5. Jumping to Final thoughts.

Extrapolating a negative thought to a larger and broader scale from a small experience. As an example: He told me he did not want to go out with me. My life must be miserable because I am unlovable.

6. Magnification or minimization

Taking credit for other people's success (or happiness) while minimizing your own achievements and flaws. I messed up at the game, but Susan had an entirely different experience.

7. Emotional Reasoning

When you assume your negative feelings reflect the truth.

Example: I felt embarrassed, therefore I must have been acting in an embarrassing manner.

8. Should statements.

You blame yourself when you don't do something differently.

The best thing I could have done was keep my mouth shut.

9. Labeling and mislabeling.

It happens when you assign yourself a huge, general label based on a small adverse event or feeling. My report was forgotten. A complete idiot, I am.

10. Personalization.

Personalizing things that shouldn't be personal. Dinner, for example

My presence at the party made it bad.

How to Use the 5-minute Triple Column Technique

Using the triple column exercise can help you identify and correct 10 of the most common cognitive distortions.

Although it can be done in your head, I have found that writing it down really helps you to get rid of the negative voice that's in your head.

Here's how you do it:

On a sheet of paper, create three columns, or use Google Sheets or Excel to create a spreadsheet. It is possible to beat yourself up whenever you want to, or when you notice you are doing it. Some people write theirs before bed to clear their minds, but I prefer to do it in the morning when I'm feeling anxious.

As you begin writing in the first column, Burns suggests turning to what he calls an "automatic thought." This is what you call your negative self-talk, that little mean voice in your head. It doesn't matter whether you're brief or detailed. I had a bad workday, which may be the title of yours. Unfortunately, my presentation bombed, and my boss hates me.

In the second column, write the cognitive distortions you have observed in your statement (observing it in print can be somewhat shocking). One may be present or there may be more than one. Our example illustrates four of them: overgeneralization, all-or-nothing thinking, mental filters, and jumping to conclusions.

The third column should contain your "rational response," a reflection of your thoughts and feelings based on logic. For example, you could have written, My presentation could've been better, but I've had a lot of successful presentations in the past. There's a good chance I'll talk to my boss tomorrow about directing the presentation and how it could've gone better. No evidence exists to suggest that I would be fired if I had one subpar work day.

There is no limit to the number of automatic thoughts you can write. A good day might leave you with no worries, and a stressful event or conflict might leave you with a lot.

With time, I've learned I'm better able to spot my own distortions and know that my negative talk is at best illogical. In the worst case scenario, it is exaggerated.

And is it proven to work?

Despite its effectiveness as a standalone treatment for anxiety, anger, and stress, a 2012 meta-analysis of 269 studies found that this simple talk therapy is even more successful when combined with other treatments. Complete the triple columns to your heart's content!

Mary Curry

POSITIVE SELF-TALK: HOW TALKING TO YOURSELF IS A GOOD THING

- Benefits of self-talk
- Identify the negative
- Examples of positive self-talk
- Practice daily
- Takeaway

WHAT IS POSITIVE SELF-TALK?

Your internal dialogue is your self-talk. Your subconscious mind influences what you think, believe, and act out.

Positive and negative self-talk are both possible. You can find encouragement in it, as well as distress in it. Personality greatly influences how you speak to yourself. You may have a more hopeful and positive self-talk if you are optimistic. In general, if you tend to be pessimistic, the opposite is true.

It's possible to manage stress effectively by thinking positively and being optimistic. Positive thinking can indeed lead to some benefits for your health. Optimists, for example, had a better quality of life, according to a 2010 study.

The inner dialogue you can use to shift your mindset can be negative or positive depending on your need. It can make you more positive and it can help you become healthier.

WHY IS IT GOOD FOR YOU?

The practice of self-talk can help you perform better and be more healthy. Self-talk has been proven to help athletes improve their performance, for example. Their endurance may be improved or their ability to deal with heavy weights may be enhanced.

Furthermore, positive self-talk can have other benefits for your health, including:

- Enhanced vitality
- A higher level of life satisfaction
- Enhanced immunity
- Pain reduction
- Improved cardiovascular health
- Better physical health
- Death risk reduced
- Less distress and stress

Positive self-talk and optimists may also experience these benefits, but the reasons are unclear. Positive self-talk, however, appears to enable people to solve problems, think differently, and be able to cope with hardships and challenges more effectively. It can reduce the harmful effects of stress and anxiety.

How does it work?

Identifying negative thoughts is the first step to practicing more self-talk. In general, self-talk and thinking fall into four categories:

1. **Personalizing. You are always blaming yourself.**

Magnification. Ignoring any and all positive aspects of a situation, you only focus on its negative aspects.

2. **A catastrophizing attitude. If logic or reason tries to convince you otherwise, you tend to expect the worst.**

Polarizing. The world appears black and white to you, or good and bad. It is impossible to categorize and process life events in the middle.

You can begin to convert negative thinking into positive thinking as soon as you recognize your negative thinking patterns.

It takes practice and time for this skill to develop. You can do it, which is good news. Children can even correct their negative self-talk, according to a 2012 study.

WHAT ARE SOME EXAMPLES?

Below are examples of how negative self-talk can be transformed into positive self-talk. Practice makes perfect. In these examples, recognizing your own negative self-talk can help you learn how to flip the thought.

Negative: I will disappoint everybody if I change my mind.

Positive: I have the ability to change my mind. Other people will understand.

Negative: I embarrassed myself and failed.

Positive: I feel good about myself for even trying. It took courage to do that.

Negative: I am overweight and in poor health. It might be better not to bother.

Positive: I am capable, strong, and want to get healthier.

Negative: My failure to score let down everyone on my team.

Positive: Sports are a team event. Together, we win and lose.

Negative: I've never done this before and I won't be good at it.

Positive: I'm looking forward to learning from others and growing from this experience.

Negative: This will never work.

Positive: I can and will work my hardest to make it work.

HOW DO I USE POSITIVE SELF TALK ON A DAILY BASIS?

When you don't have a natural ability to talk positively to yourself, it takes practice. It is possible to learn to make your inner dialogue more positive and encouraging, especially if you are generally more pessimistic.

It takes time and effort to form a new habit. It is possible for your thoughts to shift over time. It is possible to become accustomed to positive self-talk. You can help yourself by following these tips:

Identify the traps of negative self-talk. In certain situations, you may experience self-doubt and more negative self-talk. Organizing work events can be challenging, for instance. By determining when you tend to think negatively about yourself, you can prepare and anticipate.

Feel out your feelings. If you're experiencing a bad day or an event, stop and listen to yourself. Does it have a negative trend? Where can you make a difference?

Discover the humor. Stress and tension can be relieved by laughter. When your self-talk needs a boost, watch funny animal videos or listen to a comedian.

Positive people should surround you. No matter what you are thinking or feeling, you are absorbing the outlook and emotions of the people around you. Negative and positive people are included, so choose positive people whenever you can.

Affirm yourself positively. Sometimes, all you need is a piece of positive writing or an image to inspire you. Whenever you spend significant amounts of time at work, at home, or elsewhere, place reminders.

When should I seek support?

Positivity in self-talk can lead to a better outlook on life. As well as improved health, it can result in improved quality of life and well-being. A lifetime of self-talk will eventually create a habit.

Changing your negative self-talk and pessimistic mindset is possible if you are prone to it. Positivity can be developed with time and practice.

Taking the time to talk with a therapist could help you achieve success. You can learn to switch the switch off by seeking mental health expertise. Ask a friend or family member to suggest a therapist, or ask your health care provider for a referral.

HOW TO CHANGE NEGATIVE THINKING WITH COGNITIVE RESTRUCTURING

- How does it work?
- Techniques
- Self monitoring
- Questioning assumptions
- Gathering evidence
- Doing a cost-benefit analysis
- Finding alternatives
- Benefits
- What it helps
- Drawbacks
- Bottom line

Negative patterns of thought are common, but sometimes they become ingrained enough to affect relationships, achievements, and even wellbeing.

An important element of cognitive restructuring is recognizing negative thought patterns and changing them.

The idea of interrupting and redirecting destructive and self-defeating thinking is a good thing to do when they occur. It is possible to achieve this through cognitive restructuring.

How does cognitive restructuring work?

CBT focuses on cognitive restructuring, an approach to talk therapy that has been shown to be effective for treating a wide range of mental health disorders, including depression and anxiety.

Cognitive behavior therapy (CBT) seeks to reshape negative thought patterns by identifying faulty thoughts that contribute to the problem and discussing techniques to help do so.

You may have difficulty recognizing your own errors in thought patterns. As a result, most professionals advise you to seek the help of a therapist if you wish to begin cognitive restructuring.

The name of the technique suggests it deconstructs unhelpful thinking patterns and rebuilds them accordingly.

There are times when people suffer from cognitive distortions, which create an unhealthy view of reality. People suffering from cognitive distortions are often depressed, anxious, have relationship problems, and engage in self-defeating behaviors.

Some examples of cognitive distortions include:

- Black-and-White Thinking
- Catastrophizing
- Overgeneralizing
- Personalizing

When we restructure our brain we become aware of these maladaptive thoughts in real time. Then, you can refine your thoughts in a more helpful and accurate way.

You may be able to alter your feelings and actions if you can change how you view certain events or circumstances. So how exactly do you restructure a negative thought?

COGNITIVE RESTRUCTURING TECHNIQUES

Many people find it helpful to collaborate with a therapist rather than use cognitive restructuring techniques alone to improve their thinking habits.

Your therapist can help you identify your cognitive distortions. In addition, they can describe reasons for irrational or inaccurate thinking.

In addition to helping you get rid of faulty thought patterns, a therapist can help you redesign them so they are more positive.

Here's a brief guide to some of the strategies involved in cognitive restructuring:

Self-monitoring

A person must be able to identify the errors they are making in order to change their thinking style. To conduct cognitive restructuring, you will have to become aware of your negative thoughts and feelings.

As well as noting where and when the thoughts arise, it's helpful to notice when they're occurring. Depending on the situation, it may be more likely that you have cognitive distortions. It may be helpful to know what these situations are in advance.

An example is a student with anxiety who tends to catastrophize in testing environments. You might think something like this: I will definitely fail this test, I will fail the course, and I won't be able to graduate with the rest of the class. I will be known to everyone as a failure.

You can catch your negative thoughts before they get out of control by knowing that vulnerability exists.

As part of this process, some people like to journal. It may help you see a cognitive distortion or pattern, even if you aren't sure at first what's caused your anxiety or sadness.

As you practice self-monitoring, you'll probably become more aware of distorted thinking patterns.

Questioning your assumptions

In addition to cognitive restructuring, one of the essential components of living a productive life is learning how to question their thoughts and assumptions.

By using the Socratic method, a therapist may be able to pinpoint and explain your biases and illogical beliefs.

Some questions you might ask include:

- Is this thought based on emotion or facts?
- Is this thought supported by evidence?
- Does this thought have any evidence to support it?
- Is this belief testable?

- Is there anything worse that could happen?
- What would I do if the worst happened?
- Is there any other way to interpret this information?
- Do we really have a black-and-white situation here or are there some shades of grey?

For example, you might assume the worst outcome if you are experiencing the cognitive distortion known as catastrophizing. Consider listing all possible outcomes as an alternative to this thought pattern. The likelihood of each outcome could be determined by asking yourself this question.

If you ask questions, you can consider possibilities that aren't as catastrophic as you may fear.

Gathering evidence

Cognitive restructuring involves gathering evidence.

In addition to who you were with and what you were doing, you may choose to keep a record of events that trigger a reaction. If you want to remember how each response was, you may want to write it down.

In addition, you might collect evidence to support or refute your theories, assumptions, or beliefs. It is important to recognize that cognitive distortions can be both biased and inaccurate, as well as deeply rooted. They can only be dislodged and replaced if there is evidence that they are rational.

If you see a belief as accurate, compare it to facts that prove it to be distorted or incorrect.

As an example, if you choose to personalize the actions of other people, you may often blame yourself for things that aren't your fault. If you want to understand how an action has no bearing on you, you should examine evidence that indicates that.

Performing a cost-benefit analysis

This strategy would allow you to weigh the pros and cons of keeping a particular cognitive distortion.

You could ask yourself:

- When you label yourself an idiot, what do you gain?
- Can you quantify the emotional and practical costs associated with this thought pattern?
- How long-term are the effects?
- What impact does this thought pattern have on those around you?
- Is it advancing your career or limiting it?

Consider the pros and cons of changing the pattern side by side so you can make an informed decision.

As an example of a cost-benefit analysis in action, here's a recent celebrity example:

Hannah Gadsby shared her career-building experience in her show "Nanette." The harm she was doing to her self-confidence outweighed her career benefits at some point. So she stopped humiliating herself to make jokes.

Many people recognize that they make harmful trade-offs every day, which is why "Nanette" was wildly successful.

Generating alternatives

Through cognitive restructuring, people are able to see things from a new perspective. In the practice, we come up with alternative explanations that are rational and constructive to replace the distortions that have become entrenched over time.

Instead of generalizing that you are bad at math because you did poorly on a test, you may look at ways you could improve your study habits. Alternatively, before your next test, you might want to try some relaxation techniques.

A second example: If a group of colleagues freeze up when you walk into the room, instead of thinking they are talking about you, consider other explanations. By doing so, you may realize you did not cause the situation or that you misinterpreted it.

It's also possible to create positive affirmations that replace inaccurate or unhelpful thought patterns when creating alternatives.

Often, your colleagues will include you in what's happening at work, and you always make a valuable contribution to them. Based on what you've actually accomplished and the positive relationships you've forged, you can make these affirmations.

What are the benefits?

Cognitive restructuring is something you can learn on your own once you're aware of how it works, even though it's helpful to start working with a therapist.

Understanding how you think has many benefits, including the ability to change it. Consider, for instance:

- Stress reduction and anxiety reduction
- Build stronger relationships by improving your communication skills
- Substance abuse should be replaced with healthy coping mechanisms
- Self-esteem and confidence must be rebuilt

What are some of the problems that cognitive restructuring can resolve?

CBT is recommended to help with:

- Mood disorder
- Anxiety
- Worry
- Post-traumatic stress disorder
- Alcohol and drug abuse
- Psychological problems
- Mental illness
- Marital problems

In addition, it can help you cope when you are going through difficult transitions, such as a divorce or a serious illness.

You can challenge and change unhelpful thoughts through cognitive restructuring in any situation where negative thought patterns develop.

Are there any drawbacks?

As cognitive restructuring typically involves working with a therapist, potential drawbacks might include the out-of-pocket fees for therapy sessions.

Mayo Clinic doctors have noted that medication combined with CBT techniques can be most effective in some cases.

The bottom line

Cognitive behavioral therapy includes cognitive restructuring as a core component.

Collaboration is a key component of cognitive restructuring most of the time. Patients work with therapists to identify and replace problematic thought patterns with healthier ones.

Mental health psychologists believe that cognitive restructuring may reduce symptoms of anxiety, depression, and other mental health difficulties.

HOW TO TALK BACK TO YOUR INNER SELF-CRITIC

1. Name it

2. Meditation

3. Step back

4. Journal

5. Professional help

Each of us experiences health and well-being differently.

At some point in their life, everyone struggles with self-esteem. We're often the worst critics of ourselves, as the saying goes. Careers aren't the only area where this is evident; it can be seen in all areas of our lives.

My blog is dedicated to mental health and I hear from readers everywhere about the struggles of self-talk that holds them back.

It is not we who think, but the person who listens to them.

Many of us find it difficult to push back the negative voices that nag us, and yet when they are left unchecked, they can really take their tollHere are some tips for changing the channel on the radio in your mind if it always seems to be playing the song "I'm the worst".. There are some ways to get the radio in your head to change stations if you find yourself listening to the "I'm the worst" song over and over again.

1. GIVE THAT CRITICAL, MEAN VOICE IN YOUR HEAD A NAME

Several of my friends have shared with me how they tried to combat the negative voices in their head that had skewed their thinking by giving them a name: Brian.

Brian, why? It's an anagram of the word "brain", they told me. Clever, yes, but it's also a powerful reminder that our thoughts don't define us - we are simply going through them.

No matter what you hear that critical voice called, be sure to not identify with it or place too much significance on it. Imagine you are the one who filters the thoughts, deciding which ones to hold onto and which ones to let go of.

Negative, self-defeating thoughts should be removed from your mind as much as possible.

There is no way to choose your thoughts, but you can strive to maintain a healthy distance between yourself and them. Self-critical statements - such as not being smart or good enough - should be acknowledged when you hear them.

Your response might be, "Thanks a lot, Brian." In order to affirm that it isn't necessarily true, we ask questions and flip them around:.

- Are you a failure as a result of that mistake, or are you just imperfect like everybody else?
- Did your boss's outburst really reflect your inadequacy, or was it a reaction to a bad day at work?
- Can it be that your friend is too busy to reply back to you, or does he just not like you?
- The world looks different when you slow down.
- Even if we don't question our thoughts, we could forget that they are only thoughts.

2. TRY OUT A GUIDED MEDITATION

In the course of my life, I went through a lot of trauma that led to a lowered sense of self-worth. After my experience, I let the pain

I felt define me as someone unworthy of protection, safety, or service.

As a result of a friend's suggestion, I decided to practice meditation to cope with trauma. It surprised me how much it helped me, given my skepticism at first.

I was able to be gentler with myself when I used this framework. This was important to me since I have always been impatient with myself, wondering why I couldn't just "get over" my past trauma. The recovery process requires trust, and a breach of trust is often the cause of trauma.

My traumatic experiences taught me negative ideas about myself, so once I realized these, I was able to rewrite my brain's negative mental script.

Meditation has countless benefits, both for physical and emotional health, so I should not be shocked - after all, there are countless advantages to meditating. There are now more apps to choose from than ever before, so getting started is easier than ever.

3. LEARN HOW TO TAKE A STEP BACK

If I am beating myself up over something, I often ask myself, "What would I say if my friend was experiencing the same thing?""

Keeping things in perspective can be easier if we are able to practice self-compassion. If you could put yourself in someone's shoes, who would it be? Can you support them in any way?

However, not everyone is naturally inclined to do this. When I have trouble with this, Wysa helps me tremendously. A team of psychologists and designers created an interactive chatbot that acts as your personal life coach. Through the application of artificial intelligence, it challenges self-defeating thoughts and behaviors using different behavioral therapy and self-care techniques.

With Wysa, for instance, you learn to identify what is known as cognitive distortions, or the lies we are told by our brains.

It's possible that you're assuming fault or overgeneralizing when it's not necessary. Wysa can help you identify patterns such as these, see where it is not useful or accurate, and come up with new ways of thinking about an issue or event.

The Wysa chatbot can help you keep things in perspective if you need it.

4. Start Keeping a Journal

Journaling can be a great way to get things off your chest. Journaling isn't just cathartic; it's also a great way to become more self-aware. Writing regularly helps us combat negative thoughts because we're not always aware when they're happening.

The exercise of making a two-column journal has been very helpful for me. Throughout the day, I check the first column for any criticism I receive from myself.

I take a moment to review the notes I've compiled into that column, then rewrite them in an empowering or positive way.

Rather than writing, "I made an error at my job," it would be more appropriate to write, "I learned how to do something better at my job, which will help me improve."

My skin looks gross today, so I might rewrite that as, "My outfit today was amazing, but I wasn't happy with my skin."

While practicing and rehearsing self-esteem might sound corny, it remains true. We can learn to shift our perspective by finding a space in which to change our attitude such as a journal.

5. Consider finding a therapist

In the case of persistent negative thinking - adversely impacting your functioning and quality of life - it could be an indication of something more serious.

A therapist or psychologist will be able to help you address these issues if you have them accompanying issues like depression, anxiety, low motivation, fatigue, hopelessness, and more.

Mental health conditions such as depression and anxiety don't always respond to positive thinking and keeping a journal. Sometimes getting a fresh perspective from an unbiased outsider can completely change your perspective. The following resource can assist you in deciding what therapy option is best for you if you aren't sure if you can afford it.

If we don't naturally do something, we can feel a little silly when we try it for the first time. The situation won't last forever, however. You need to be patient with your self-esteem when it comes to boosting it. But It is always worth the effort to maintain your mental health and wellness, and I hope you find that it comes with a little practice.

Having a positive self-image and self-esteem can impact your happiness level as well as your stress level. As an example, if you trust you are able to handle new situations, difficult situations will tend to be viewed as challenges rather than as threats; conversely, if you do not trust yourself to handle new situations, they will likely be viewed as challenging and stressful. Having a sense of self-efficacy contributes both to self-esteem and stress management.

KNOW YOUR WORTH

WHAT IS THE MEANING OF SELF-WORTH AND SELF-VALUE?

There is a close relationship between self-worth and self-value, and they are commonly used interchangeably. In order to feel worthwhile, one must value themselves, and in order to feel valuable, one must value oneself. In general, the terms refer to the same concept, but there are some minor differences between them.

In order to feel valuable, one must value oneself, and in order to feel worthwhile, one must value themselves.

Self-worth is defined by **Merriam-Webster** as:

"a feeling that you are a good person who deserves respect".

Self-value, on the other hand, is more behavioral than emotional, and is more about how you behave in relation to what you value, including yourself, rather than how you feel about yourself" (Stosny, 2014).

THE PSYCHOLOGY OF SELF-WORTH

Self-worth might not be one of psychology's most popular topics, but that doesn't mean it's any less important. A person's sense of self-worth is at the core of how they view their value, worth, and worthiness. Their thoughts, feelings, and behaviors are influenced by this view.

WHAT IS THE SELF-WORTH THEORY?

Those who believe in self-worth believe that achieving success in life is the key to finding self-acceptance (Covington & Beery, 1976). Compelling others is often the key to achieving success.

Therefore, it is logical to conclude that competing with others can boost our sense of accomplishment, which leads us to want to feel proud of ourselves and feel more accepted.

A self-worth model consists of four main elements:

1. Ability
2. Effort
3. Performance
4. Self-worth

A person's self-worth is affected by these four factors in conjunction with one another. Performance and feelings of worth are influenced by one's ability and effort.

It is unfortunate that we place so much emphasis on our achievements when it comes to understanding self-worth. A sense of self-worth can stem from a multitude of factors, including competing and "winning" against others.

WHAT DETERMINES SELF-WORTH?

According to the self-worth theory, self-worth is mainly determined by how we evaluate our abilities and how well we perform certain activities that we deem valuable.

Nevertheless, people often measure their worth by other criteria. People use five top factors to measure their own worth and compare it to others' worth:

1. Appearance, be it by weight, clothing size or attention received from others;
2. An individual's net worth can be measured by their income, wealth, material possessions or financial assets;
3. People judge the worth of themselves and others based on who they know and what influential and influential people they know;
4. You are judged by what you do or your career - for instance, a stockbroker is often viewed as more

successful, valuable, and valuable than a janitor or a teacher;

5. Achievements-we value people's worth based on their achievements (whether our own or another's), such as success in business, etc performance on the SAT, or placement in an athletic event (Morin, 2017).

6. Throughout her book, Stephanie Jade Wong (n.d.) attempts to correct misperceptions and misconceptions about self-worth. The following are factors that do not determine your self-worth (or should not determine your self-worth) instead of listing all the factors that go into it:

- **The to-do list:** Achieving goals is wonderful, and crossing things off the list feels great, but it has no direct relationship with your value as a person;

- **Your job:** There is no right or wrong job. You should do it well and fulfill yourself through it;

- **Social media following**: It also doesn't matter how many people follow you or retweet you. Even though considering the perspectives of others can be valuable and enlightening, their opinions cannot change our intrinsic worth;

- **Your age:** You're never too young or old for anything. It doesn't matter how old you are, since your age has no bearing on your worth as a human;

- **The opinion of others:** or what they have done, is irrelevant. The things you think, say, and do are not nearly as important as what others think, say, and do for you;

- **Running distance:** Running time is not one of the most important factors to your self-worth (or your worth in general). It's good for you if you're happy to improve your time while you run. You're doing well if not! Self-worth does not depend on how fast you can run;

- **Our grades:** Everyone has different strengths and weaknesses, and some of us simply aren't cut out to do well in class. There is no difference in worth between Straight-A students, straight-F students, or dropouts, and this does not affect our value as people;

- **Number of friends:** Your worth as a human has absolutely nothing to do with having a lot of friends or connections. Relationship quality is what matters most;
- **Your relationship status:** If you are single, in a dating relationship, or in a committed relationship, your value remains unchanged; whether you are single, dating casually, or in a committed relationship, you are worth the same;
- **You are who you are**, no matter how good you look, how sophisticated you are, or how refined you are. It doesn't matter how you measure your worth.
- **The only person who determines your self-worth is you**: Nothing or no one else matters to you. A person who believes they are worthy and valuable is also worthy and valuable. It doesn't matter whether you believe you're valuable and worthy or not-you are!

3 EXAMPLES OF HEALTHY SELF-WORTH

Perhaps you're thinking, "Okay, I know what does and does not (and shouldn't) determine self-worth, but what does healthy self-worth look like in reality?"?"

Here are a few examples of the determinants of self-worth.

Alec is a bad student. Even when he studies a lot, he gets most of his grades as Bs and Cs. It wasn't a good SAT result, and he's not a great reader, writer, nor mathematician.

Alec is happy even though he doesn't have the best grades. It doesn't matter how good his grades are; his character is just as valuable as his straight-A friends. A realistic view of Alec's abilities and self-worth is a highlight of his personality.

Now let's take a look at Katrina. Katrina enjoys taking part in marathons, reading, attending book clubs, playing trivia with her friends, and making new friends.

It isn't Katrina's strength but rather her lack of ability to run that causes her to consistently fail in marathons. Her book club members pick up on symbolism and themes that she misses because she reads slowly. Her friends often help her when she does not know the answer to a trivia question. Unsurprisingly, she does not answer every question correctly. Lastly, she enjoys talking to new people, though she is sometimes ignored and blown off.

Despite all this, she continues to believe she is valuable and worthy. No matter how well she can run, read, play trivia, or make new friends, her value as a human is not dependent on these abilities. She knows that, despite her success, failure, or somewhere in between, she deserves happiness, fulfillment, and love as long as she excels at each of her many choices of hobbies.

Last but not least, we have Tom. Despite being an excellent salesman, Tom almost always ends up behind one of his coworkers. In addition to playing squash, he regularly competes in the sport tournaments. Sometimes he places first or second, but more often than not, he doesn't place.

No matter how bad he is at his job or what he enjoys doing, Tom is still proud of himself. Despite not being the smartest, most talented, or most successful, he thinks he is smart, talented, and successful.

Alec, Katrina, and Tom are confident in their own abilities. Each of them has different abilities and talents, and they accomplish a wide range of things with their efforts, but no matter what they accomplish, they understand that what they do doesn't define them. The high opinion of themselves as a person persists regardless of whether or not they win awards.

HOW TO FIND SELF-WORTH AND VALUE YOURSELF MORE

If Alec, Katrina, Tom sound appealing to you, there is hope and you can be more like them. The best way to boost your self-worth is to see yourself as a complete, wonderful human being who deserves respect and love no matter what.

HOW TO BUILD SELF-WORTH

In order to develop lifelong traits, one should begin young. Don't forget to encourage adolescents to accept and understand their own worth. Make them feel valued instead of "doing," as some say—in other words, ensure they understand that their value comes from who they are, not from what they do.

Check out the following suggestions for specific ways that you can boost an adolescent's self-esteem.

Two main strategies are recommended by researchers at Michigan State University:

1. Give positive regard, unconditional love, and respect;
2. Give adolescents the opportunity to succeed (Clark-Jones, 2012).

The best way to teach a teenager self-worth is to show him unconditional love (if you're a parent, family member, or very close friend) or unconditional respect and positive regard (if you're his teacher, mentor, etc.).

Teenagers will learn that it's okay to love themselves for who and what they are if you show them that you love and appreciate them. She is less likely to limit her self-love and self-respect if you demonstrate she does not need to earn your love and respect.

In addition, positive experiences early in life contribute to a healthy sense of self-worth. The feeling that we feel good about ourselves increases when we have successful experiences.

Having successful experiences often opens the door for taking healthy risks and achieving success. Give teens every opportunity to succeed, so they believe they are worthy and valuable.

If these opportunities are really meant to help her succeed on her own, make sure they are genuine ones---giving her a helping hand is fine, but we should be able to build a healthy sense of self-worth on our own as well (Clark-Jones, 2012).

HOW TO INCREASE SELF-WORTH AND SELF-VALUE

While it may be more challenging to increase self-worth and self-value , it's certainly not impossible. Learn how to get started with the following two tips.

First, review what doesn't determine self-worth. It shouldn't matter how many followers you have on social media, your bank account, or your job title to how valuable or worthy you are.

When determining someone's worth, take a step back and look at their actions, their generosity, compassion, empathy, and kindness to others.

In the second stage, identify, challenge, and externalize the critical voice inside you. Firestone (2014) explains that every individual has an inner critic who is always finding fault with them. It's natural to Let our inner critic win sometimes, but if we let her win too often, she will begin to believe that she is right!

You should pause when your inner critic attacks with criticisms whenever you notice her. If she tells you something, ask yourself if it is a matter of fact, whether it is in your interest for her to tell you, and whether it is something you need to know. Please tell her to go out if any of those things aren't true!

Make her realize that no matter what you do or do not do, you are worthy and valuable no matter what you say or do.

In later parts of this piece, we will cover exercises, activities, and worksheets with more specificity.

THE IMPORTANCE OF SELF-WORTH IN RELATIONSHIPS

A common mistake people with low self-esteem make is relying solely on one aspect of their lives to define their self-worth -- the one they are in currently.

I understand the tendency to let someone else's love for you influence your self-esteem. Regardless of whether you are in a romantic relationship or not, you should feel good about yourself.

You can't define yourself by the love of another person, or by the value you place on yourself. The value of being single, casually seeing someone, building a lasting relationship, or simply you should give yourself time to practice self-compassion and self-acceptance as you celebrate your 30th wedding anniversary with your spouse.

In any relationship status, this can be true, but for long-term partners it may be particularly important.

The love of your partner does not make you lovable. You don't want to be forced to start over if anything happens to your partner or to your relationship. Breakups and grief can be made much harder when this is present.

While these facets of the issue might be enough to motivate you to improve your self-worth, there is another reason it would be beneficial: It will improve your current relationship.

Learning to love yourself makes it easier for you to love others. They know that they must first find their own worth, esteem, and happiness within themselves before they can have satisfying, loving, and stable relationships.

Those who have self-worth and are happy from within are much brighter than those who are trying to absorb the light of one another (Grande, 2018).

THE RISKS OF TYING YOUR SELF-WORTH TO YOUR JOB

It is dangerous to tie your self-worth to your job in the same way that tying it to someone else can be dangerous. Job opportunities come and go, sometimes without notice, just like a significant other.

We can let you go, lay you off, transition, dehire, dismiss, downsize, reroute, release, selectively separate, terminate, replace, ask you to resign, or just plain fire you. It is also possible to be transferred, promoted, demoted, or given new duties and responsibilities that do not align with what you value about yourself.

If you base too much of your self-worth on your job, quitting, taking a new job, taking some time off, or retiring can also be unnecessarily challenging motions in your life.

The job you have does not define your worth or who you are. It's fine to be proud of your work, to find joy or fulfillment in it, or to let it shape your identity; the danger comes when it becomes all you are.

The work we do is just a small part of who we are. It is detrimental to our well-being and devastating during tough times to think we are simply a job.

THE SELF-WORTH SCALE

Is it important for you to know how much value you place on yourself? Luckily, you've come to the right place. This curiosity is well suited to a certain scale.

This scale, which was developed in 2003 by Crocker, Luhtanen, Cooper, and Bouvrette, is also known as the Contingencies of Self-Worth Scale. It measures self-worth across seven different domains through 35 items. An example of each item in these seven domains is:

1. Achieving approval from others (i.e., it doesn't matter if others don't like me);
2. I am affected by my physical appearance (i.e., how attractive I think my face or facial features are);
3. Competing better than others (i.e., my self-worth is affected by how well I do when I compete with others);

4. Academic ability (i.e., I feel bad when my grades are low);
5. The love and support of my family members (i.e., it does not affect my self-worth how well I get along with them);
6. Following my moral/ethical principles (i.e., whether or not I am virtuous or moral);
7. The love of God (i.e., my self-esteem would suffer if I did not have His love).

Ratings range from 1 (strongly disagree) to 7 (strongly agree). Divide the five items from each domain by five to calculate the subscale score once you have rated them.

ACTIVITIES AND EXERCISES FOR DEVELOPING SELF-WORTH

Adam Sicinski, an author and self-growth guru, says there are five key exercises for increasing self-worth. Several stages are outlined, but there is no need to stick to a strict order. You can revisit them or move from stage to stage if you wish.

1. Increase your self-understanding

Building self-understanding is an important step on the road to self-worth. Becoming a worthy human being begins with learning who you are and what you want.

To improve your understanding of yourself, Sicinski recommends the following simple thought experiment:

1. Think about losing everything you own (i.e., possessions, relationships, friendships, status, job/career, accomplishments and achievements, etc.);
2. Consider these questions:

a. Is it possible to lose everything I have in an instant?
b. Would I still be myself if it was just me left?
c. How would that make me feel?
d. Which of my possessions would actually be valuable?

1. If you answer these questions, you may discover that you are not affected internally by external events or by anything taken away from you;
2. Here are some questions you can use to get to know you better:

    a. Who am I? It's me. . . I am not . . .
    b. How am I doing?
    c. Is the world fair to me?
    d. What do others think of me?
    e. What do others say about me?
    f. What key life events have shaped who I am today?
    g. What are my greatest passions, fulfillment, and joys?

1. It's time to take a hard look at what isn't so great or easy about being you once you have a good understanding of who you are and what fulfills and satisfies you. Consider these questions:

    a. How do I struggle the most?
    b. What needs to be improved?
    c. How do I overcome my fears?
    d. How do I feel hurt by my habitual emotions?
    e. How often do I make mistakes?
    f. What tends to let me down consistently?

1. Consider the flipside for a moment; ask yourself:
    a. What are my abilities?
    b. What do I really excel at?

Pay attention to each step, but primarily those that remind you of your own value and worth (e.g., the strengths step).

2. Boost your self-acceptance

Knowing who you are will help you accept yourself better once you have a more complete picture.

If you listed anything in item 5 above, start by forgiving yourself. Consider any struggles, areas of improvement, mistakes, and bad habits you have, and put yourself in a position of forgiveness and acceptance without judgement or excuses.

In the first exercise you learned a lot about yourself. Repeat the following statements:

1. Good, bad, and ugly, I accept them all;
2. The parts of me I'm not proud of, such as my flaws, fears, and behavior, are all accepted without reservation;
3. I am comfortable with how I am

3. Enhance your self-love

Once you have accepted yourself as you are, you can begin to care for and love yourself. Set yourself the goal of being kind, tolerating, generous, and compassionate.

Start paying attention to how you speak to yourself in order to boost your self-esteem. Make a commitment to speaking to yourself more positively and uplifting.

Try thinking (or saying) these simple statements if you're not sure how to start:

1. I feel valuable and special;
2. My love for myself is unconditional;
3. My worth and capability are apparent (Sicinski, n.d.).

4. Recognize your self-worth

Knowing, accepting, and loving yourself will allow you to no longer depend on people, accomplishments, or other external factors for your self-worth.

Now is a great time to recognize your value, appreciate what you've done to get here, and maintain your self-knowledge, self-acceptance, self-love, and self-worth.

You deserve to feel good about yourself if you:

1. It is not necessary to please others anymore;

2. The way you feel about yourself is determined by you alone, regardless of what others do or say;

3. Based on your internal sources and resources, you are able to respond to events and circumstances and resourcefulness, reflecting your real worth;

4. Value comes from within, from a standard you've established for yourself.

5. Take responsibility for yourself

This stage will train you to be responsible for your own circumstances and your own problems.

For the best results, make sure you follow the following guidelines:

- Do not surrender your power or your agency to others without taking full responsibility for your own actions;
- Recognize your personal power to influence and change events and circumstances in your life.

As you reflect upon all of these exercises, take a moment to appreciate what you have learned. Don't lose sight of your well-earned self-worth and ensure that it is maintained.

4 WORKSHEETS THAT HELP INCREASE SELF-WORTH

Not to worry if you prefer to complete structured activities and exercises instead of more freeform ones. You can build your self-esteem with these four worksheets.

ABOUT ME SENTENCE COMPLETION WORKSHEET

To develop self-worth, follow the steps in this worksheet. Only a pen or a pencil are needed and it only takes a few minutes.

As the worksheet's title suggests, it is about writing about yourself: a sentence completion activity.

Complete the following sentence stems (or prompts):

- When . I was really happy. . .

- I am liked by my friends because . . .
- The work I've done for me is something I'm proud of. . .
- I made my family happy when I . . .
- When it comes to work, I'm good at . . .
- I am unique in that I . . .

Self-Esteem Checkup

Young children, adolescents, and older adults can all benefit from this worksheet. Although self-worth and self-esteem are used interchangeably in the opening text of the worksheet, it is a self-esteem worksheet.

By completing this worksheet, you will gain an understanding of your own respect, acceptance, and love for yourself.

You are asked to rate your belief in 15 statements on a scale from 0 (not at all) to 10 (completely or totally). As follows:

My belief in myself;

There is no difference in the value of me and others;

The person I would rather be is me;

I am proud of my achievements;

Whenever I get compliments, I am happy;

Criticism is not a problem for me;

It is easy for me to solve problems;

I enjoy trying new things;

Self-respect is something I value;

It's nice to look at myself;

It doesn't matter how others treat me; I love myself no matter what;

Positive attributes I possess;

Success trump's failures for me;

I am not afraid of making mistakes;

I'm glad to be me.

After adding up all of the ratings for these 15 statements, rate your overall self-esteem on a scale from 0 (I dislike myself completely) to 10 (I truly appreciate myself).

Respond to the final prompt, "What is the one thing you would need to change for you to move up one rating point?"? How would you be able to reach a 7 if you rated yourself as a 6? (i.e., what would you need to do in order to reach a 7?)"

My Strengths and Qualities Worksheet

If you or someone you know is young, you can use "My Strengths and Qualities" as another opportunity to work on boosting self-understanding, acceptance, love, and a sense of self. Sense of worth. The worksheet could not be easier to complete-all you need is a pen or pencil and a few minutes.

There are three spaces to respond to each of the eight sections; however, feel free to indicate more than three points.

The sections are:

1. What I am good at;
2. My favorite aspect of my appearance;
3. In helping others, I have;
4. This is what I value most;
5. Compliments I've received;
6. Challenges I've overcome;
7. I am unique because of these things;
8. People have been happy because of me many times.

WORRYING IS WORTHLESS

"Don't worry about tomorrow, for tomorrow will take care of itself," Jesus said. *Each day brings its own troubles" (Matthew 6:34 NIV)*. Due to your emotional energy spent regretting what has already happened and fretting about what will happen tomorrow, you ended up messing up today.

However, worrying does not change anything. Worry is pointless! It cannot change the past. The future is beyond its control. You will only be unhappy today if you worry. You waste every minute of your life worrying.

In worry, you place your trust in yourself rather than in God. It's a form of atheism. You act like an orphan when you worry. You're You act as if you don't have a God who promises to care for you. I think you're thinking you need to deal with your problems on your own. Your focus will need to change if you want to break that habit of worry in your life. You can draw closer to God by fasting and praying. Fasting is an abstinence from something that allows you to let your needs draw you to God.

Focus must be chosen. By thinking your way, you are likely to feel fearful, anxious, and worried. Because of your sinful nature, you're going to have anxiety. The Spirit of God resides in you when you are focused on Him and don't worry. It leads to life and peace.

The secret to overcoming worry is not to say, "I won't worry." That isn't going to work, as you are focused on the opposite.

Changing the channel is the key. You can't resist it. *Focus*. You can trust God's love and promises when you focus on him.

Although it is difficult to stop worrying, you should change your mindset to thwart this type of behavior. Several ways are available for you to do so:

Work on changing your outlook to be more positive. Expecting good things makes us more likely to get them and we're less likely to worry.

Concentrate on building your confidence. You will have a more positive outlook on life if you believe in yourself, and you will be better able to handle circumstances that don't go as planned (perhaps reducing the worry factor overall).

Learn to embrace failure. The silver lining of a negative outcome is that it often is a learning opportunity. Our mistakes always lead to better outcomes, so we learn from our mistakes. When you learn to accept that things may not work out right away, you will become less stressed.

Why worry? Do you enjoy worrying?

"No, I want to stop worrying...."

Then try these tips on how to stop worrying:

- Do you admit your worries or do they come from reality? An example would be worrying about what other people think and then trying to conform to their expectations.
- Focus on finding a solution rather than getting trapped in thoughts about the problem.
- You may wish to seek advice from a well-wisher if you cannot complete the task.
- Keeping your mind on the tasks at hand will not only keep you out of trouble in the present, but also in the future.

- When you cannot see a solution to a problem that seems beyond your control, why worry? Keep trying and remain positive.

God said, "Don't panic, even when adversity strikes."

Worry is like a fire. There is a constant fear of something bad happening. Dadashri said, "Awareness is caring, while worry is anxiety that eats you up from within." Since stress and worries are not external but are, essentially, internal problems, the solution for becoming worry-free would be to understand who the true "doer" is. Self-Realization and discovering the science behind doership are the first steps to gaining this knowledge.

WORK ON YOUR OPTIMISM

It can be beneficial to your self-esteem and overall happiness to be able to see the glass as half-full. Additionally, there are numerous proven benefits to optimism, so cultivating positive habits of thinking in order to become more optimistic can benefit your health as well as your general happiness. In order to develop optimism, you need to affect your self-talk and change your focus in order to identify the types of worldview that you adopt.

How to train yourself to have an optimistic mindset

It is important to learn how to supply this reservoir, which functions as a reservoir in our minds. Positive thinking is an attribution style; it is how we interpret the world around us.

Pessimistic and optimistic people will see the world differently when evaluating a fact of life.

Positive Facts: "I received a raise!"”

Profile: I am always optimistic.

Profile of the Pessimist: My taxes will go up even more.

A negative fact: "I lost my key to my home."

Profile: I never lose anything, they probably got picked up by someone else.

As a pessimist, I am always distracted and forget everything!

You shouldn't be discouraged if you identify with the pessimist profile. Then you will be able to make the best of any situation with mental strength and daily training.

Whenever you speak, avoid negative phrases like "I can't," "I give up easily," or "I am *insert negative adjective here*". As an example, you may have heard yourself say, "I'm lazy." A better way to put this would be, "I'm not effective today.". In order to accomplish all of my tasks, I will create a list tomorrow." Additionally, try to avoid complaining at all costs. It is better to view a challenging client as a positive challenge than as a negative experience. As a result, you'll be able to help the client efficiently and with good spirits.

It is also helpful to write down any positive events that happened to you during the day, no matter how small they are. You might wish to record in your journal that you helped an organization manager lower their stress level. Be sure to take a picture or write down any particularly stunning gardens you see. Record the highlights of the conversation with your team if it was productive. If you do so, you will train your mind to look for the positive in your surroundings. Always keep an open mind to practicing and learning about optimism.

DEVELOP POSITIVE SELF-TALK

It is believed that a person's "self-talk," or how they talk to themselves and interpret things, can significantly affect their self-esteem. It is dangerous to adopt a habit of thinking down about life and yourself because it can lead to a negative perspective. Learn how to alter your self-talk to a more positive outlook, helping you to see yourself and society more positively.

- Do You Think You're An Optimist?
- You perceive yourself and your world differently based on the thoughts you have. Find out your level of positivity or negativity!
- Stress and Negative Self Talk
- You use self-talk to view the world, explain situations, and communicate with yourself, and it can affect your stress level depending on whether you use negative or positive self-talk. Find out why and how to change.
- Self-talk that is positive
- You can negatively impact your self-concept when you talk to yourself negatively.

TRY NEW CHALLENGES

Self-esteem can be boosted simply by becoming involved in hobbies. Being aware of what you are good at can change your self-perception and boost your self-esteem. In addition to enhancing your happiness, hobbies can relieve stress as well.

STAY AWAY FROM TOXIC PEOPLE

Sometimes we all feel down, but some people can build you up instead of tearing you down, and those people can destroy your self-esteem more than you might imagine. The key to regaining self-esteem is recognizing the drainers of our self-esteem and establishing boundaries. In addition, developing more supportive relationships can provide us with enormous support. Create a social life that you deserve.

Mary Curry

TALKING IT OUT

Freely expressing your feelings and emotions is considered a relatively superficial act; however, it can provide temporary relief and open the door to deeper therapy. When stress-stricken or emotionally disturbed individuals express their problems and concerns in the presence of an understanding listener, they report gaining a sense of relaxation and comfort.

There are many therapists who have encountered the experience described by Maslow and Mittelmann (1941): A woman who came in for an interview talked for fifty minutes straight about her problems, then got up to leave, remarking, "Thank you doctor, you helped me tremendously." During the psychiatric discussion, a patient is expected to talk extensively, but the involvement goes far beyond letting him vent about his conscious difficulties.

Patient-centered therapy or non-directive therapy encourages patients to speak freely about anything that comes to mind-though talking is only one part of therapy. The therapist's ability to reflect back a patient's own thoughts and feelings is crucial to his progress, as it allows the patient to begin to perceive himself differently, to adjust his attitudes and aims, and to realize his own inner potential.

Psychoanalysis, too, emphasizes talking out, even though it is often called "the talking cure." Although talking is essential, the goal is to have the patient talk about what is innermost in his mind, not what is exterior. However, the process goes much beyond catharsis or merely letting go of emotions, because it is meant to uncover those hidden Understanding a patient's unconscious motives and emotions can be used to bring about fundamental change. Only this way can basic change be achieved.

By analyzing dreams and free association, a psychoanalyst attempts to explore what lies beneath the surface and see how past experiences relate to present struggles. Hence, the analyst realizes that the key to therapeutic success may lie in what the patient cannot express. Thus, he must come up with inventive ways to overcome the patient's resistance to obtain significant information. In general, speaking out frequently may provide a patient with a sense of relief, but it does not necessarily result in healing. In addition to paving the way to genuine treatment, its major value lies in its effectiveness.

WRITING IT OUT

However, writing goes way beyond that. Putting words on paper is what makes us writers, even if we don't have the skill level of Faulkner. A writer's greatest asset is his or her ability to think, express, and create; the cabin dweller be damned.

Here are some of the benefits of writing regularly.

Writing and happiness

Writing about what you think and how you feel is a common theme in research on writing and happiness. In terms of therapeutic value, blogging "undoubtedly offers similar benefits" as private expressive writing.

Regular expression of the self can lead to improved moods, well-beings, and reduced stress levels, according to Adam Grant:

According to Laura King's research, people who write about achieving their future goals and dreams are happier and healthier in the long run...

Writing and communicating clearly

Lack of words makes it difficult to describe feelings, share experiences, and communicate with others. It is extremely frustrating to be able to construct thoughts in your head only to have them ramble out at the very last minute. There seems to be some respite provided by regular writing.

The ability to write effectively has been demonstrated, both in the hard sciences like mathematics, as well as in emotional intelligence.

Creating a written piece forces you to decide what you want to say; prose enables you to ignore fuzzy abstractions, meaningless words do not.

Writing and handling hard times

According to a study that followed recently fired engineers, those who consistently engaged in expressive writing found another job more quickly. Says Adam Grant:

In written reports, the engineers reported feeling less anger and hostility toward their former employers. Furthermore, less alcohol was consumed. Compared with the control group, less than 19% of engineers remained full-time eight months later, while more than 52% remained full-time."

The emotional benefit of writing about traumatic events did not take hold until about 6 months after the event. This is according to an older study.

Participants reported, "I finally managed to work through the pain, rather than blocking it out, despite not talking about what I wrote. I don't think it hurts to consider it now."

Timing appears to be crucial for the impact of expressive writing. If writing is an activity that is engaged in naturally, the benefits appear clear, but forcing the process can only worsen things.

Writing and gratitude

Study authors noted that when subjects were given an opportunity to write down their positive experiences once a week, they were more positive and motivated about their current situations and about their future.

The problem was that they benefited little from writing about them every day. I can see why this would make sense; if you do something too much, it can feel phony and boring. Gratitude should be reflected on and written about regularly rather than begrudgingly often.

Writing and your "mental tabs"

How many tabs do you have open at once on the Internet? Often, when the brain is trying to juggle a lot of thoughts at once, there are too many tabs open at once.

When you write, you give form to your ideas, free up bandwidth, prevent browser crashes, and put your ideas onto paper.

You can eliminate the stress associated with losing your thoughts to time or a cluttered mind by writing important ideas down.

Even though I may have made notes or outlined an idea, I have never felt inclined not to work on it-in fact, I'm more likely to carry on with it since it has already begun.

You can always rely on Mitch Hedberg's joke: "I sit in my hotel at night and think of a joke I want to tell, then pick up a pen and write it down."

Writing and learning

We learn best when information is presented as though it needs to be taught or rewritten in our own words. Until I started writing regularly, I did not really grasp the concept of a "writer's ear.".

In order to create a piece of written work that is interesting, an individual must be receptive and focused on discovering new sources of inspiration, insight, and information. Besides reading books, listening to podcasts and watching videos, I have also listened to podcasts and listened to radio so I could learn something new so I can write about it later.

Curating good ideas encourages you to think more deeply, research more, and look for new perspectives on topics you are interested in. The ability to deal with big ideas is aided by having a large volume of work.

After writing on a particular topic for some time, you'll be able to build on earlier thoughts, utilizing what you've already written to develop new ideas - in our industry, we have seen more than a few people who regularly write support emails turn a sentence from one of their customer conversations into an essay, which eventually led to a book.

Writing as leadership at scale

Although we may now be drowning in a sea of personal brands, there are some truly exciting opportunities that a "anyone can publish" world presents.

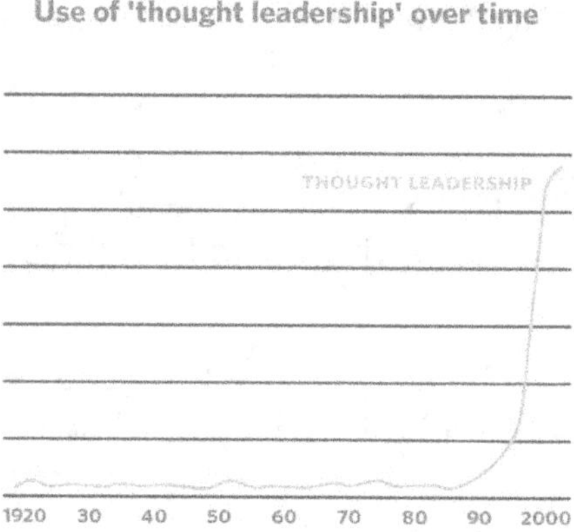

By using only your words, you can leave a large impact. Once someone emails you saying they liked your work and how it helped or influenced them, it is a bit of a shock.

There is no doubt that the positive feedback for "leadership at scale" motivates the writer as well.

Few others learn to build thick skin the way writers do. The breakfast of champions is criticism, even if it is unjustified.

Mary Curry

PHYSICAL EXERCISE AND STRESS

It is inevitable that we will experience stress in our lives. In the United States, seven out of ten adults experience stress or anxiety daily, and most report at least moderate interference in their lives as a result. Stress and anxiety disorders were the most common causes of death in the most recent ADAA survey. In a 2008 survey by the American Psychological Association, more people reported physical symptoms due to stress compared to 2007, with nearly half reporting an increase in stress over the past year.

In most cases, stress cannot be eliminated, but it can be managed. ADAA online poll shows that 14 percent of people regularly exercise to relieve stress. The rest spent time with friends or family (18%), sleeping (17%), watching movies (14%) and eating (14%) as well as listening to music (13%).

Although all of these techniques are well-known, health care professionals often recommend exercise as the best. One of the best ways to exercise is to walk (29 percent), run (20 percent), and practice yoga (11 percent) according to ADAA poll participants.

EXERCISING BODY AND MIND

In addition to its physical benefits -- improving health and reducing disease risk -- exercise has long been recommended by physicians. In addition to keeping a healthy mental outlook, exercise can help reduce stress. According to studies, it reduces fatigue, improves alertness, improves concentration, and improves overall performance cognitive function. As a result, These methods can be especially useful after you have been stressed and are not able to concentrate.

Because the brain is surrounded by many nerve connections, stress affects the entire body. Therefore, it is obvious that when you feel better physically, you will feel better mentally as well. Exercise produces endorphins - chemical messengers in the brain that reduce pain - and also improves sleep, which, in turn, reduces stress. The result is the release of endorphins by your body when you meditate, undergo acupuncture, or even breathe deeply. According to conventional wisdom, low- to moderate-intensity exercise gives you energy and makes you feel healthy.

The participants of aerobic exercise have shown to lower overall levels of stress, elevate and stabilize their mood, improve their sleep, and improve their self-esteem. Exercise can help alleviate anxiety even after just five minutes.

How DOES EXERCISE HELP DEPRESSION AND ANXIETY?

Exercise may relieve depression and anxiety in the following ways: By releasing feel-good endorphins and other neurochemicals like cannabis (endogenous cannabinoids), as well as by increasing your sense of well-being.

Avoiding negative thoughts that trigger depression and anxiety by removing your mind from worries

The benefits of regular exercise extend to psychological and emotional well-being as well. Here are some things it can help you with:

Build your confidence. Reaching a goal or meeting a challenge, no matter how small, boosts your confidence. Feeling good about your appearance can also be improved by getting in shape.

Increase your social interaction. It is possible to meet new people through physical activity and exercise. Changing your mood from day to day just by smiling or wishing others well can lift you up.

Take care of yourself. It is healthy to take positive steps to cope with depression or anxiety. It is possible for depression and anxiety to worsen when people drink alcohol or dwell on how they feel.

RELATIONSHIP OF EXERCISE TO ANXIETY DISORDERS

The United States is home to 40 million adults with anxiety disorders, the most prevalent mental illness. Exercising may provide health benefits beyond stress relief, such as improving anxiety disorders.

Exercise, according to psychologists, can relieve anxiety and depression in the same way as a 45-minute run workout. Exercising quickly can lift a depressed mood, according to some studies by many people. It shows that a brisk walk, for example, can relieve a headache for several hours, like taking an aspirin.

The scientific community has also indicated that physically active people tend to be less depressed and anxious than those who are sedentary. By making the brain more resilient to stress, exercise may benefit mental health. In one study, researchers found that those who started exercising regularly during their early twenties were more likely to develop depression or anxiety within the following five years.

EXERCISE AND STRESS: GET MOVING TO MANAGE STRESS

Stress can be reduced by exercising in almost any way. You may be able to block daily worries and feel good after being active.

Although you know exercise improves your health, you're often too busy and stressed to make time for it. There is some good news regarding exercise and stress.

Almost any exercise, from yoga to aerobics, can be a stress-relieving activity. Even if you are not an athlete, you can benefit from some exercise even if you are not in shape. Learn the exercise as the key to stress relief - and why you should include it in your stress management program.

EXERCISE AND STRESS RELIEF

As a result of exercise, you stay healthy and feel better, so you're more energetic and motivated every day. However, exercise can also reduce stress directly.

It pumps up your endorphins. The feel-good neurotransmitters in your brain, called endorphins, are boosted by physical activity. In fact, any form of aerobic exercise, including tennis or nature walks, can produce this same effect.

It reduces the negative effects of stress. Your body can benefit from exercise by creating stress-like effects, such as the flight or fight response, and practicing working together through those effects. Additionally, by helping protect your body from harmful effects of stress, it can have positive effects on your cardiovascular, digestive, and immune systems.

It's meditation in motion. You will often find that you have forgotten the day's irritations and are only focused on your body's movements after playing racquetball, taking a long walk or running, or swimming laps. Through regular movements and physical activity, you may begin to find that you are able to reduce your daily tension. When you are calm, clear, and focused in everything you do, you will have more energy and optimism.

It improves your mood. Self-confidence, mood improvement, relaxation, and lowering anxiety and mild depression symptoms can be contributed to regular exercise. Stress, depression, and anxiety can also disrupt your sleep, so exercise can help. The benefits of exercise can help you deal with stress and feel more in control of your life and body.

HOW DOES EXERCISE REDUCE STRESS AND IMPROVE MOOD NATURALLY?

Anxiety can be treated naturally with physical exercise. In addition to keeping the muscles relaxed, it also encourages a positive mood and improves your mental capacity.

Stress can be relieved and mental health improved by exercising:

1. Focusing your mind on physical activity instead of your worries can help you relax.
2. Resulting in endorphin release,
3. By creating new neural pathways in the brain, you can break unhealthy thought patterns
4. Anxiety is caused by inflammation (research shows this), so reducing inflammation is important
5. Exercise that relaxes you (at the end of or during the exercise),
6. The key to decreasing anxiety and stress is getting an adequate amount of sleep (for more information, see my earlier post Sleep And Anxiety- A Cyclic Relationship),
7. Enhancing your body's natural ability to respond to stress and to hormones such as cortisol and adrenaline,
8. Increasing your comfort with an increased heart rate (so that anxiety does not compound the issue by anxiety about your heart rate),
9. Increasing your self-confidence
10. The stress-tense muscles need to be worked.

PUT EXERCISE AND STRESS RELIEF TO WORK FOR YOU

Simple steps are the key to a successful exercise program.

Consult with your doctor

You may want to talk to your doctor about starting a new exercise routine if you haven't worked out in a while or if you have medical concerns.

Walk before you run

Gradually increase your fitness level. It is possible to overdo a new program and to even get injured. Most healthy adults should get 75 minutes of vigorous activity or 150 minutes of moderately intense aerobic activity each week, according to the Department of

Health and Human Services or a combination of moderate and vigorous activity. Examples of Exercises that are moderate in aerobic intensity, such as walking or swimming, as well as exercise that is vigorous, such as running or biking. Even greater benefits will be achieved if you exercise more. Try to engage in strength training two to three times a week.

Do what you love

Fitness and stress can be reduced by almost any form of exercise. What matters most is that you choose something you enjoy. You can walk, climb stairs, jog, dance, bike, practice yoga, Tai Chi, garden, lift weights and swim.

Don't forget that you don't need a gym membership to get moving. Make a yoga video, do body-weight exercises, or take a walk with your dog.

Pencil it in

On some days, you may work out in the morning and do an activity in the evening. Making exercise an ongoing priority requires committing to moving every day. Exercise should be a part of your weekly schedule.

STICK WITH IT

The first step toward a healthy lifestyle is to start exercising. Following are some tips to help you stick with a new exercise routine or revitalize a tired one:

Set SMART goals

Create SMART goals - specific, measurable, achievable, relevant, and time-bound. You should specifically focus on reducing the amount of stress in your life if that is your main goal. Having a day each week that you will walk during lunch might be a goal for you. Try exercising at home by watching online videos. Consider hiring a babysitter so that you can attend a cycling class without having to worry about your children.

Find a friend

Having someone eagerly awaiting your arrival at the gym or in the park can be a powerful motivator. Plan walks or workouts with your friends. When you exercise with a friend, coworker, or family member, you are more motivated and committed to your workout. It can be fun to exercise with friends!

Change up your routine

Take a look at other, less competitive options like Pilates or yoga classes if you're a runner who needs stress relief. Plus, you'll also enjoy a decreased stress level after these kinder, gentler exercises.

Exercise in short bursts

Efforts to be physically active, even for a short time, can be beneficial. You could, for instance, walk for a few minutes instead of one 30-minute walk if you can't fit in one. It is possible to gain health benefits from being active throughout the day. Go for a walk or perform squats or pushups during a mid-morning or afternoon break.

The brief (60 to 90 seconds) bursts of intense activity at near maximum effort that are part of interval training may help you gain the same benefits as longer workouts without the risks and drawbacks of exercise. Maintaining a regular physical activity routine is a crucial style.

No matter what you do, don't look at exercise as just one more thing on your to-do list. Making an active tennis match part of your routine will help you stay healthy. If you prefer meditative strolls down to the park, then that is the activity for you. You can unwind and reduce stress by engaging in a variety of physical activities.

The following exercises will help you relax and reduce stress

1. Yoga

Why it works to reduce stress: Yoga postures increase physical endurance and flexibility, and thus relieve tension in the body. As well as deep breathing, it triggers the body's relaxation response.

According to studies, yoga can also reduce blood pressure.

One of yoga's greatest benefits is the improvement of mental focus. Stress can be managed by focusing on what is important.

The poses are meant to require concentration, according to Boston-based yoga teacher Noel Shroeder, who created the *Notice Your Experience* DVD (yinward.com).

How to do it: Yoga classes are available at gyms, studios, and community colleges for all ages, temperaments, and fitness levels.

As an example, hatha yoga is gentler and emphasizes stress relief, whereas power yoga, vinyasa yoga, and Bikram yoga are more athletic classes.

It is also possible to practice yoga at home on your own.

2. Tai Chi

Why it works to reduce stress: Taiji (also called Tai Chi Chuan) is a Chinese martial art that links movement with the breath.

Tai chi is often referred to as "meditation in motion," as it encourages a focus on the moment - a mental absorption that allows everyday worries to dissolve.

In addition to increasing flexibility and energy, Tai Chi improves one's overall well-being.

In addition to improving balance and sleeping better, it can also aid in improving cardiovascular fitness.

How to do it: Unlike yoga, Tai Chi poses are linked with each other and your breath; there are no pauses between them. Tai chi comes in several styles that differ in intensity.

These classes are offered by community colleges, wellness centers, and senior centers. To learn how to do Tai Chi at home, try Tiffany Chen's DVD, Step by Step Tai Chi.

3. Qigong

Why it works to reduce stress: Acupuncture, herbs, and qigong are all part of traditional Chinese medicine. Qigong is no different.

Regularly practicing qigong will relax you, improve your sleep, your digestion, and increase your energy.

In the same way as tai chi, qigong helps people be aware of their bodies, says Migdow.

His practice of concentrating on breathing and slow, gentle movements calms the nervous system.

How to do it: There are a number of senior centres, community centers, and YMCA's that offer Qigong.

4. Walking

Why it works to reduce stress: You don't need special equipment or classes to do it.

Walking is good for heart health, blood pressure, cholesterol, and type 2 diabetes, and can reduce the risk of many stress-related conditions.

The act of walking also reduces stress and boosts confidence. It deepens breathing and quiets the nervous system as well as releasing tension. "We also get to enjoy nature."

How to do it:

If you're just starting out, walk for 10 minutes twice a week as an exercise.

You should gradually increase your walking frequency and duration after two or three weeks.

For maintaining health and managing stress, walking for 30 minutes a few times a week is usually recommended.

You'll need to walk longer than average when you have the time (maybe 90 minutes on Sundays) and/or more intensely (perhaps take a hilly route or increase your pace). Heavy breathing is acceptable as long as it does not feel labored.

Start by visiting our Walking Guide.

5. Gardening

Why it works to reduce stress: You can actually exercise while gardening.

Those who weed alone may burn up to 200 calories an hour, and those who perform more strenuous duties, like hauling bags of dirt or raking, may lose up to 600 calories an hour.

It also provides you with a chance to be in touch with nature, a stress-buster that rejuvenates your spirit.

How to do it: Take it slow. You can feel more connected to nature by growing a few herbs on a sunny windowsill.

You might consider getting a primer, like Gardening Basics for Dummies, produced by the National Gardening Association.

6. Dancing

Why it works to reduce stress: In addition to its physical benefits, dancing has many psychological advantages as well. As you work out, your grace and agility will improve because of the increase in heart rate.

The researchers have noted that ballroom dancers are less likely to develop dementia, perhaps because they are constantly learning new steps.

Additionally, dancing builds social connections and a sense of community among people, resulting in lower stress levels and greater happiness.

How to do it: No matter what you prefer, the choice is yours. There are studios such as Arthur Murray or community centers where you can enroll in a class.

Free classes are usually offered before dance and music events at many clubs. Taking part in a hike requires only comfortable shoes and an adventure-seeking attitude.

7. Circuit Training

Why it works to reduce stress: Weight-training moves alternate with cardio moves in circuits, and there are short breaks in between.

Hence, you get the same results in a shorter amount of time as a longer exercise session (30 minutes or less).

This short and sweet exercise enhances your mood by pumping up your endorphin levels. Even better, there will be no worries about finding time to workout.

How to do it: During an exercise circuit, members are guided by musical cues to switch stations as part of Curves' circuit training program. A DVD from fitness diva Kathy Smith, Super Slimdown Circuit, is an even cheaper option.

8. Pilates

Why it works to reduce stress: Exercises in Pilates emphasize body awareness, tight abdominal muscles, and proper alignment.

"Pilates creates a physical harmony by simultaneously strengthening and lengthening muscles that makes stress less likely to settle in," states Ellen Barrett, fitness expert and designer of the Pilates DVD *Slim Sculpt*.

Pilates demands intense mental concentration, which keeps you absorbed in the present, Barrett says.

Also, Pilates has been known to reduce back and neck pain, a side effect of stress.

How to do it: The Pilates Reformer machine, usually found only in Pilates studios, can also be used on the floor on a mat (and will be labeled as "mat" in gym timetables). If you want to try Pilates at home, check out the DVD Pilates for Beginners.

9. Tennis

Why it works to reduce stress: Tennis is an excellent cardio exercise that prevents high blood pressure, heart disease, and other stress-related disorders. Because tennis cannot be played alone, it helps you stay connected to others - a key factor in stress reduction.

Workout on a tennis court triggers your body to release endorphins. The biochemicals that produce pleasure and satisfaction are those involved in euphoric feelings," explains Lifescript's Personal Coach, John Sklare.

How to do it: Taking lessons is advised if you are new to the sport and want to learn proper form. Lessons and leagues are available at many city parks. Join a private group if you regularly play (or want to) tennis club. If you join a tennis community, you can access a tennis community at a lower cost than a country club.

EXERCISE AS PART OF THERAPY

Several studies have shown that regular physical activity can reduce anxiety and depression symptoms for some people as well as medication, and those effects tend to last for a while. Exercise can significantly reduce symptoms in a short period, and can alleviate them for hours at a time.

In general, exercise is beneficial for mental health, however, some studies indicate that exercise may not be beneficial to those with anxiety or depression or who may not benefit from it long-term.

As with all forms of therapy, the result can vary from person to person: Some may experience a positive feeling, others may not, and others may only experience a modest short-term benefit. Yet when it comes to exercising for bodily health, researchers say there is no dispute, and people should engage in physical activity.

WHAT IS MEDITATION?

Meditation is a means of experiencing the love, peace, and stillness that is within us. We experience it by focusing our attention within instead of on the world outside and by taking it away from the world outside. By doing so, we can detach from the turmoil of the world and connect with God, the Source of all love and joy. We carry a reservoir of untapped love within ourselves, and meditation is the highest form of prayer.

A person's love for God can be expressed through meditation.

WHAT IS SOS MEDITATION?

At Science of Spirituality, the technique of meditation called SOS is designed to help people experience the inner Light of God. People of all ages, faiths, and beliefs can practice it. The focus of this form of meditation is on what is called the spiritual eye, which is between and behind the two eyebrows. It is from this seat of the soul that we enter the inner spiritual realms. We get to the point where our sensory currents focus there and we open into the inner realms of the spirit.

WHAT HAPPENS DURING SOS MEDITATION?

A spiritual Master can provide complete meditation instructions that will allow you to experience various forms of Light and spiritual realms. The consciousness or soul enters higher regions when you focus your attention on whatever appears before you with your eyes closed. Higher and higher levels of Light are found in successive regions. Ultimately, a soul must return to the place from which it came in order to find all-consciousness and all-light. As a result, they show us the mysteries of life and death and provide knowledge and wisdom. This gives us a sense of peace and bliss that can't be replicated in this world.

Meditation Heals the Body

MEDITATION REDUCES STRESS AND ANXIETY

Throughout the world, people have turned to meditation to relieve stress and anxiety as research has shown that meditating regularly and accurately can reduce anxiety and stress. In turn, this reduces the risk of diseases associated with stress, such as heart disease, digestive disorders and headaches, while alleviating stress-induced illnesses like high blood pressure, insomnia, chronic pain and fatigue.

MEDITATION INCREASES IMMUNITY

As well as improving recovery after surgery and illness, meditation increases resistance to disease. Mediation is thought to have these health benefits because it allows the brain waves to slow down to a state of calm, which in turn allows the body to become calmer and more relaxed.

MEDITATION REDUCES PAIN

The majority of hospitals and medical centers now offer meditation classes for reducing stress, eliminating certain illnesses, and improving patients' health. By healing our emotions and our minds through meditation, we can heal our bodies. Our attention is diverted from feeling the effects of illness when we become absorbed within. By shifting our consciousness from our physical bodies to our spiritual sides, we can access the Divine's healing power. In meditation, we can transcend physical pain by connecting with the power within ourselves.

MEDITATION RELAXES THE BODY

Meditation provides us with greater rest than sleep. How? Sleep is when we dream. Sometimes we dream of good things, and sometimes we dream of stressful things. As if awake, the sleeping body may respond to dreams. Sleeping may cause tossing and turning. Meditation, however, is a state of stillness of the body and the mind. In meditation, we cannot react to stressful thoughts or dreams. Therefore, it is a peaceful time for our body.

MEDITATION HEALS THE MIND

Pressures often cause our minds to be agitated. The world has become increasingly complex. The number of things people have to do is increasing while the number of hours in the day is decreasing. It is possible to work too many hours and take on too much responsibility. They are also raising families while working two jobs. Some people snap - they become irritable, off-balance, and feel stressed. Their behavior may be uncharacteristic of them. Sometimes they take out their frustrations on family members.

MEDITATION CALMS THE MIND

By practicing meditation, you can eliminate the stress-induced lack of balance. Our minds are restored to equilibrium by spending time in meditation. The brain waves that are recorded by researchers range from 13 to 20 Hz during times of stress work, driving in traffic, or in a fight-or-flight time. When in a state of deep relaxation, the brain registers between 8 and 10 Hz, as it does during meditation. Reduced stress levels result from meditation. Calming the mind calms the body, and the body, in turn, becomes calm. Meditation heals the mind. We can then live in peace and function more effectively in this world.

MEDITATION IMPROVES CONCENTRATION

Taking care of our daily needs with less stress increases mental clarity, equilibrium, and balance. Focus and concentration are enhanced, increasing productivity in all our endeavors. Conflict and adversity can be faced with ease and equanimity when we are in control of our reactions. The angle of our vision shifts. Our perspective on life changes when we see what it is for what it is.

MEDITATION HEALS THE EMOTIONS

In modern society, meditation is regarded as a solution to a variety of ailments. What is it that makes it so effective?

Understanding the underlying causes of many ailments is also important. Do we feel these emotions because we cannot cope, are unfulfilled, lonely, disconnected, or hurt? We may seek connection or healing in our lives; perhaps we are afraid or feel unsure about who we are or how we fit into the world. Our view of life's glass is perhaps distorted. No matter what their causes are, they have one thing in common: they all originate from our environment.

Throughout our lives, we have sought love because it is our true nature. Our love for ourselves is experienced in meditation.

Meditation Bathes Us in Love

The healing power of meditation can be used in conjunction with therapy. Meditating helps people to increase their healing as they seek help from specialists for emotional problems. There are several benefits to meditation. To begin with, rising above body consciousness helps us to see our lives clearly. By recognizing the root of our pains, we can solve them. A second benefit of meditation is that it connects us with the universe of love. Love, consciousness, and bliss are the same elements that make up the Current of Light. We experience divine love throughout our contact with the divine current. Our connection with God is latent in us. God is love, our souls are love, and we can only return to God through love. Godly love can open us to a depth of love that we have never imagined. You may be able to fill the emotional hole that is at the core of your pain. It is possible to minimize and even eliminate mental pain through meditation.

Meditation Improves our Communications

Our relationships with the outer world are improved through communicating with the inner world, which is a form of meditation. As we experience higher realms of existence, we find that the Light within us is within other people.

It provides a deeper understanding of life's unity. In this way, we develop love, tolerance, and respect for people of all backgrounds. The way we view life and how we behave begin to change as a result. Through this, we learn to care about others and treat them with kindness. Helping and serving people is what we aim for. As much as possible, we strive to eliminate other people's suffering. We will become kinder and more humble, empathetic, and compassionate.

Can Meditation Help Me Cope With Life's Problems?

Many of life's problems are out of our control, and they will always exist. The benefit of meditation, however, is twofold: (1) It can help us control the unhealthy physical responses we have to challenges. Our hearts beat slower during meditation, and our bodies and minds relax. During times of calm, the body's physical reaction to stress is moderated. By meditating, we can protect ourselves against stress and deal with problems without affecting our physiological systems. Our reactions can be controlled through meditation. (2) Meditation changes our perspective on life, so we begin to see everything from a new viewpoint. The result is a calm and poised response to problems.

Meditation Eliminates the Fear of Death

Throughout meditation, the soul appears to us to live on after it has left the body. This experience confirms that life continues after death. Changing states of existence is what death is.

It is similar to taking our coat off. Our physical gestures are thrown away for our spiritual ones. Regardless of our physical bodies' death, we are eternal. As we age, we lose our fear of death. In facing life's challenges, we can find inner peace through this. With a calm attitude and wisdom, we deal with life in a way that makes others feel at ease.

Meditation Can Become Our Inner Retreat

Meditation, once we become accustomed to it, can be used in difficult situations to provide the same calming effect. It would be better to take a moment to meditate before reacting. By meditating, we prevent ourselves from reacting in ways that trigger stress. When tension arises in the day, the calm of a meditative state can help calm us. Meditating more often can help us gain a greater sense of serenity as we face challenges every day.

Spiritual Benefits of Meditation: The Real Reason to Meditate

Although these benefits are important, they are merely byproducts of true meditation. Meditation is not as simple as it seems. It is to reap the spiritual benefits of meditation that one should meditate - it is for this reason that we should meditate. Through meditation, we become aware of our true essence, our spiritual nature. In order to gain knowledge of God, we must discover our spiritual nature first, and everything else that follows falls into place. We experience the love, the joy and bliss we were born to seek, and this love seeps deep into our very being. It feels good to be at peace with ourselves.

Inner and Outer Peace

We, however, are not the only ones who benefit from meditation. In addition to the numerous benefits of meditation, we also begin to radiate the love and peace we feel while meditating back to others just like a flower diffuses its scent. In our healing experience through meditation, each of us becomes a messenger of God's love, allowing the world to heal. Love and peace become our ambassadorial duties. Meditation leads to inner peace, which contributes to peace in our world.

YOUR DIET & STRESS

Chronic, unremitting stress does more than just give you headaches and stomach cramps, or make you gain weight and catch the cold or flu more often. Chronic stress affects every aspect of your body, from your digestive system to your reproductive system. The National Institute of Mental Health (NIMH) reports that chronic stress may even lead to conditions such as obesity, type 2 diabetes, heart disease, depression, and anxiety if it is not treated.

That's right: Stress can make you fatter and sicker as well as grumpier.

HOW YOUR DIET CAN AFFECT STRESS LEVELS, FOR BETTER OR WORSE

You have some control now over your diet choices - even at a time when you may feel helpless. These factors can have a big impact on your stress level.

Here are a few things you should keep in mind about cookies and potato chips. In The Anti-Anxiety Diet, Ali Miller, RD, CDCES, says refined carbs such as these spike blood sugar, then crash it, increasing stress and anxiety. A healthy diet — including foods such as avocados, eggs, and walnuts — creates satiety, mood regulation, sleep, and energy balance by creating a favorable hormonal signal in the brain, Miller says.

You shouldn't feel guilty if you reach for the vending machine when you are stressed. Whenever you are stressed, your body releases stress hormones. These hormones boost your appetite and send cravings for the consumption of unhealthy comfort foods is on the rise, according to Harvard Medical School. The stress that you experience can result in muscle loss, a decline in metabolism, and an increased risk of weight gain.

Obviously, that's only half of the equation. Stress can affect every area of your life, from sleep to diet to exercise to family relationships to work and relationships with friends.

There is, however, a solution. We can show you how.

Our seven-day stress-busting meal plan and detailed food list are specially balanced to satisfy all of your nutritional needs while calming stress hormones, increasing feel-good hormones, and keeping you energetic. We will also give you some tips and tricks backed by experts that we hope will help you manage your stress once and for all.

Stress and time constraints may make it difficult to prepare healthy food. But this plan will pay off in a big way - and you'll likely notice the results when you're stressed out the most. In the end, you could benefit from more energy, a calmer mind, boosted immunity, and maybe even a slimmer waistline. Do we need to say more?

THE BEST AND WORST FOODS PROVEN TO AFFECT STRESS MANAGEMENT

As a result of stress, the body releases hormones cortisol, ghrelin, and insulin, which can lead to increased hunger and cravings for unhealthy foods, according to Harvard Medical School. Stressful events cause the hormones to remain elevated, increasing another hormone called leptin, It also helps you recognize when you're full. Research published in November 2010 in Journal of Endocrinology & Metabolism found that hormonal changes can raise your risk of leptin resistance, which is associated with obesity.

You can reduce your stress levels by knowing which foods to fuel up on (and which to skip).

FOODS TO EAT WHEN STRESSED

Warm, Soothing Foods

The nutrient profile of a food may be as crucial as its taste for overcoming stress. Taking a warm cup of tea is calming, according to Sandra Meyerowitz, MPH, RD, the owner of Nutrition Works in Louisville, Kentucky. It's relaxing to sip a warm drink, no matter what flavor it is, Meyerowitz notes - but certain herbs also have relaxing effects on their own. Providing rewiring of the body's stress response and increasing the production of feel-good hormones serotonin and dopamine may reduce anxiety, according to a study published in March 2013 in the Journal of Psychopharmacology.

Dark Chocolate

Chocolate is an exception when you're stressed, but not usually a good option for desserts. There are two ways in which this treat might help reduce stress - chemically and emotionally. According to Meyerowitz, chocolate can feel so indulgent that even savoring a piece of it can help reduce stress. Study participants ate about 1.5 ounces (oz) of dark chocolate every day for two weeks, and the results revealed that it could also lower levels of stress hormones. Meyerowitz recommends keeping your chocolate intake under control by avoiding overindulging. It is important to take into account the serving size when eating dark chocolate since it can add up quickly. You should consume no more than one ounce of 60 percent cacao dark chocolate per day.

Whole-Grain Carbohydrates

Attention keto diet followers who follow a low-carb diet: The right carbs can serve as stress busters. Serotonin, a chemical that helps boost mood and reduce stress, is a chemical produced by carbohydrates. According to MIT, carbohydrates contribute to serotonin levels increasing. Concentration and productivity increase when there is more serotonin in the body. Carbohydrates must be chosen wisely. Study authors believe that refined carbohydrates like chips, cookies, and crackers lead to inflammation, stress, and depression. Another study published in

Progress in Cardiovascular Diseases suggests that carbohydrates may also raise blood pressure and lead to heart problems, coupled with an increased tendency to eat more later in the day. Harvard Medical School shows that complex carbohydrates can be better for your health because they digest more slowly and maintain a stable blood sugar level. Complicated carbohydrates come from sweet potatoes and whole grains (such as whole-grain bread, quinoa, brown rice, steel-cut and old-fashioned oats).

Bananas

A banana will provide a quick boost instead of Starbucks. Dopamine, a chemical that boosts mood, is found in the yellow, potassium-rich fruit. Magnesium levels are lowered during stressful times. Researchers found that mice with magnesium deficiency also suffered from anxiety and depression in a study published in Neuropharmacology. Another benefit of bananas is that they provide B vitamins, such as vitamin B6, that help the nervous system work properly and reduce fatigue and stress, according to a Psychopharmacology study published in the summer of 2010 that examined the use of high-dose B vitamins. Furthermore, potassium bananas have been shown by Harvard Medical School to lower high blood pressure.

Fatty Fish

Boost your mood and strengthen your ticker while eating fatty fish when your heart is stressed. A review published in the Journal of Epidemiology & Community Health suggests that omega-3 fatty acids may relieve depression when consumed in whole fish such as tuna, halibut, salmon, and sardines. Study results published in Clinical Psychopharmacology and Neuroscience in August 2015 suggest that the drug may also lower overall stress and anxiety.

Water

Do you want to reduce your stress quickly and easily? Take a sip of water and fill up your cup! Hydration is important during stressful times. A study in the Journal of Sports Sciences shows that mild dehydration increases cortisol levels, causing increased stress.

Consuming enough liquids will not make your stressors go away, however this move will help protect your body from its effects when stress arises. Women need approximately 2.7 liters of water daily, while men require approximately 3.7 liters. (Around 80 percent of the hydration should come from drinks, with the remaining 20 percent coming from food.)

Milk

I think your mother was onto something when she made you consume all your milk at dinnertime. It turns out calcium could do more than strengthen your skeleton - it could also improve your mood. The December 2012 issue of Nutrition Research and Practice reported that Korean women who ate the least calcium felt the most depressed. A January 2017 study in Obstetrics & Gynecology Science suggests calcium and vitamin D, which are found in milk, may even ease perimenopausal symptoms, which can be stressful to deal with.

Nuts

A variety of health benefits come from nuts. The first benefit is that they are satiating, which means that they may prevent unhealthy cravings. Secondly, a study published in July 2012 in Hypertension found that pistachios could lower blood pressure.

The vitamin B Stress levels have also been shown to be reduced by vitamins, says Meyerowitz. Eat nuts in moderation as they are high in calories and can lead to weight gain if consumed too frequently.

Oranges and Other Vitamin C–Rich Fruits

Vitamin C does more than prevent scurvy - it can also help you cope with stress. Research published in Psychopharmacology showed that people's cortisol levels and overall stress decreased when they took 3,000 milligrams (mg) of vitamin C daily in a slow-release formula. If you want to reach these high levels, you would need to supplement with citrus fruits, such as strawberries, oranges, grapefruit, and grapes. Consult your doctor before taking vitamin C supplements.

Avocados

Feel free to guac as much as you like. As an ideal stress-busting snack, avocados are packed with monounsaturated fats, potassium, magnesium, and vitamin B6. Among the health benefits of the fruit are its potassium and vitamins C and B6. Moreover, a study published in The FASEB Journal suggests that eating avocados as a snack can help you feel sated, preventing you from eating unhealthy snacks when you're stressed.

Leafy Greens

While some may consider desk salads boring, they can be a great way to reduce stress at lunchtime. As described in a Frontiers in Psychology study published in April 2018, leafy-green vegetables, such as spinach and kale, and raw fruits and veggies are powerful stress-busters. In addition to helping to lower cortisol levels and blood pressure, leafy greens contain plenty of magnesium. Folate is also present in green leafy veggies, and it helps to produce the feel-good chemical dopamine.

FOODS TO LIMIT OR AVOID WHEN STRESSED

There are foods that are bad for stress levels, of course. The consumption of some foods (or an abundance of them) may actually make matters worse. The key to reducing stress is knowing what to include in your plate and what to leave off.

Caffeine

You could either support or sabotage your stressful levels based on how you drink coffee. It's all about volume and timing. A few cups of caffeinated beverages earlier in the day is fine, but avoid them after noon, since they disturb sleep, advises Evelyn Tribole, RD, a Newport Beach dietitian and co-author of Intuitive Eating. When taken in small quantities, caffeinated beverages like coffee and tea can assist with improving mental focus, but drinking too much may have unintended effects. When consumed in excess, caffeine can cause anxiety, nervousness, and jittery feelings of being overwhelmed," says Molly Kellogg, LCSW, CEDRD, a Philadelphia-based dietitian and psychotherapist.

Alcohol

Alcohol can equally help or harm your stress levels, depending on how much you consume. "If somebody is prone to overdoing it, alcohol is a bad idea," says Kellogg. Alcohol can actually contribute to the development of depression and make stress more difficult to manage in the long run when stress is an ongoing issue and someone continues to turn to it for comfort. Whenever you feel depressed or think you are overly dependent on alcohol, Clearview Treatment Programs advises abstaining. It's also important to remember that alcohol can contribute to many chronic health conditions. One of the leading causes of death and disability worldwide is drinking alcohol, finds a study in The Lancet published in August 2018.

Refined Sugar

Miller advises that sugar should not be used as a stress reliever. When you eat refined sugars such as those in cookies, cakes, and candy, your blood sugar rises rapidly and then rapidly drops (a phenomenon known as a sugar crash). When you are stressed and tired, you need the opposite. Increasing sugar intake may also raise depression risk, according to a 2017 study published in Scientific Reports.

STRESS-FREE GROCERY SHOPPING LIST

When it comes to grocery shopping and reducing stress, there are two parts to the equation. Firstly, planning ahead and knowing what you're going to buy at the grocery store can help you significantly reduce grocery shopping anxiety. (If your list is good enough, you may even be able to send someone else in your place?) Second, by creating a shopping list you can be conscious of the foods that will fill your home. Make sure you have healthy foods on hand so you're prepared when stress strikes!

Stress-Fighting Pantry Staples:

- Oil of olives
- There are several whole grains (brown rice, whole-grain pasta, quinoa, barley, farro, etc.) that you can eat.
- Steel-cut oatmeal (old-fashioned)
- Cacao (60%) or darker chocolate
- I especially like nuts that are unsalted (almonds, walnuts, cashews, and pistachios).
- A variety of seeds (pumpkin, sunflower, flax and chia) can be used.
- Decaf teas (in particular black, green, and chamomile)

Fresh Stress-Busting Ingredients:

- fatty fish (tuna, salmon, mackerel, trout, and sardines)
- Low-fat or fat-free milk
- Yogurt
- Sweet Potatoes
- Veggies with leaves
- Asparagus
- Berries
- Fruits
- Bell peppers
- Banana's

TIPS FOR EATING DURING TIMES OF STRESS

Eat Regular Meals

You probably already know that stress messes with your hunger signals. Fighting off a perceived threat is one of the causes, according to The Cambridge Dictionary, because the body is in fight-or-flight mode. Stress can cause our bodies to suppress hunger in the wake of fight-or-flight responses, says Tribole. As if a gas tank had broken. In this case, you may not feel hungry until you sit down, when you are already starving. If you rely on this, you may not reach your destination. Aim to avoid this effect by eating every four to five hours or so to combat this effect.

Have Healthy Snacks on Hand

It is all about preparation when it comes to stress management. Be sure to keep healthy snacks on hand if you don't have time to eat a full meal. This will prevent you from reaching for junk food. Keeping almonds on your desk, packing a banana for lunch, or storing pre-cut veggies in the fridge are all good choices.

Have a Routine (and Stick to It!)

Regular schedules can also reduce stress. By eliminating the guesswork involved in deciding what to eat, where, and when to exercise, and when to go to sleep, it makes it easier to meet your fitness goals. What's the bonus? Weight loss is possible as well. Setting daily habits and sticking to them helped people lose weight for a year, according to a small study published in Obesity Facts in December 2017. According to Kellogg, you should keep as much the same as possible each week, from the day of the week on which you shop to foods you keep stocked in the house.

Eat Mindfully

Stress is reduced when you are mindful, among other health benefits. According to a January 2018 review in PLoS One, mindfulness has been shown to reduce not only stress levels but also emotional exhaustion, depression, and anxiety. Thus, eating mindfully is essential. If your plate is in front of you, then there is no time for Instagram, Facebook, or your email. Being mindful may also contribute to weight loss, according to a growing body of research. In 2018, a study published in Obesity Reviews found that participants in mindfulness programs lost on average 6.8 to 7.5 pounds following their participation.

Be Flexible When Needed

During stressful times, don't feel guilty about allowing yourself some flexibility. You don't have to eat gourmet food every day. Maybe you eat the same thing every day for a week, or maybe you order takeout or use paper plates to conserve energy," Tribole says. Being kind to yourself and doing the best you can will help reduce your stress levels. "Nutrition is not something you attain in one week or one day - it's over a lifetime."

KEEP YOUR LIFE IN BALANCE

Everyone seems to be thinking about life balance these days. In addition to boosting your productivity, your career or business success can also be impacted by a healthy life balance. People with good balance are better able to formulate their goals, take action, and move forward in a meaningful way.

Life balance is a big question... but what does it really mean? How would we define a balanced life? We all have crazy schedules, so how do we achieve that goal?

To regain control and balance in your life, there are steps you can take to fix what is not working. As you begin seeing results, you'll be more equipped to maintain that equilibrium.

A good strategy is to experiment with small changes over time before trying to make sweeping changes. In the end, you will have acquired a whole new set of positive life habits that you will never forget!

Feeling Overwhelmed?

Everyone is so busy these days. (Say it again, right?)

Families, jobs, children's activities, and communities may all require your attention. Your attention is being fiercely competed for by all of these things.

Our schedules impose their priorities on our lives, as opposed to us setting our own schedule and priorities.

As a result, you feel exhausted, stressed, and frustrated.

You may have become off-balance in many areas, and you can create a more balanced life by taking action today.

Remember: life has more to offer than what you deal with every day.

Four signs your life may be out of balance

1. The list of everything you need to do looks like the Empire State Building
2. It seems like you're extremely busy, but you're not sure if you're achieving anything
3. The feeling of burnout is overwhelming. You're always tired, have headaches, or exhibit other physical and psychological symptoms of stress.
4. Your schedule is not your own, and you don't know where to turn.

How it feels when your life is out of balance

You may sometimes feel as if you're moving through life without any options, no purpose or freedom to pursue your highest values and priorities.

You may realize there are parts of your life you have neglected. It appears that you've focused your attention and energy on other areas instead of living your life fully.

What are your tips for bringing your life back into balance?

Follow These Six Tips To Bring More Balance Into Your Life

1.Don't try to do everything at once; accept that you can't

There are only a limited number of resources: time, energy, money, etc. It may be understandable to want to accomplish as much as possible and to please as many people as possible, but a one-man operation cannot always achieve everything.

Now, breathe deeply; regain your composure.

There is only so much you can do. Your best efforts are enough. Don't worry about being perfect, or solving all problems for all people. It is impossible to accomplish all that needs to be done every minute of every day.

That's okay.

2. Manage yourself, not time.

If you were to give up a pressing task, what would you substitute, subtract, or remove from your schedule in order to gain something more important in another area?

In order to increase your productivity, you must reduce your workload. To accomplish higher priorities, you have to be willing to let go of some activities, even temporarily.

If you are planning your week, decide what is less important and can wait. Feel the overwhelming sense of being overwhelmed disappear when these are removed from your weekly "to-do" list.

3.. Determine who "A" people are in your life.

Building up your self-esteem is their job. You are believed by them. You are supported by them. When you feel better after spending time with someone who belongs in the A category, you know they are in the category. Your life is filled with them, and you are filled with them.

A "B" person is neutral. It doesn't make any difference to you how you feel with this person after being with them.

In your "C" list, people need to be placed into a circular file, released or phased out. Obviously, that is not always the case.

These people, however, are usually a drain on your energy, causing you stress and adding to your stress level.

Add time to people or spend it with them more often. Your energy will be energized, your empowerment and inspiration will be boosted, and you will feel stronger rather than stressed!

4. Just say "No"

"Are you able to...?"".

It's just a little favor I need..."

You can always be relied upon."

"You have such a talent for..."

Listening to these messages makes you feel what? Is it flattering, irritating, or exploiting to you?

Are you worried about what would happen if you said no? Often, we state yes to things out of a sense of urgency. It is important to remember that before responding to the email you always have the right to consider what is reasonable for you to do.

You can reduce stress and balance your life by saying no to unnecessary commitments. You are also given a greater amount of power when you say yes!

5. Schedule time for yourself

In the absence of self-care, who will?

Why would anyone take the time and steps to maintain their health and well-being without you?

Our lives are enhanced when we have other people we can help, work with, be friends with, and share activities with. It is essential, however, that you first become your own best friend.

I know you want the best for your family and friends! In order to achieve that, you need to exert deliberate effort. Make sure to schedule a time and place that will let you bring the comfort, health, and joy you need right now.

In your rest, in your play, and in your growth, be intentional. Every day, spend at least ten minutes reading, walking, or relaxing. It is essential that you schedule time for yourself if you want to be at your best for your busy schedule.

6. Live with purpose!

Balance is easier to achieve when your life is centered around an authentic and passionate purpose.

It follows that you should not strive for a perfect plan that fits all.

Our lives and priorities are different, and so is the best life balance plan for each of us.

A good example of the value of maintaining a balanced life is the quote, "Life is a journey, not a destination.". In order to maintain our health, care for our children, clean our homes or achieve some goals, we do not have a "last and final time."

Despite retirement, there is always something that needs to be done, and this is a good thing!

Our lives are enjoyable when we are able to choose the activities we participate in and people we decide to be in relationships with.

Start taking steps today to regain your sense of control and life balance! Recognize when your life may be out of balance, and then take action to bring it back!

10 SIMPLE WAYS TO FIND BALANCE

Here are 10 easy ways to get results:

1. Turn It Off

Take a weekend off. It will be hard, but give it a try, even for an hour or two each night, for at least one day.

Please turn off your computer and put the phone down. Work brains need a break. Additionally, you will have more time to interact with your family and friends.

2. Trim, Trim, Trim

It's a given that you can't achieve balance and manage everything if your life is overflowing. There is no way to do it.

If it isn't essential or if it doesn't bring you anything new or worthwhile, say no. You must be ruthless!

3. Pay Attention to Your Health

Everybody says it, but we rarely do anything about it. There is a lot we need to do, but we don't make it a priority until a health crisis occurs.

Health has a direct impact on how we live and how we work. Our productivity and happiness increase significantly when we sleep enough, eat healthier, and exercise.

4. Minimize Toxins

This does not mean avoiding chemicals (though that may also help). Reduce your exposure to negative influences.

If you can't completely avoid toxic people (complainers, whiners, poor attitudes), minimize your contact with them. As much as possible, surround yourself with people who are positive, supportive, and can-do

5. Spend Time Alone

Most overworked and overwhelmed people can't make time for themselves, but doing so lowers stress, increases happiness, and increases creativity.

There are many things you can do to meditate, write, sketch, do some yoga, or simply sit quietly and do absolutely nothing every day for a few minutes.

6. Relationships Do Matter

Take time to spend with family and friends. Connect with your loved ones and pay attention instead of just watching TV.

Play a game with your child, have coffee with a friend, or go on a date with your significant other. Spend time getting to know your friends and neighbors.

7. Treat Yourself

Treat yourself to a facial or a pedicure. Make an appointment for a massage. There is no need to spend lots of money; a lovely scented candle, a glass of wine or your favorite coffee will go a long way.

8. Explore the World

Walk around and observe what's going on around you. Trying to be a tourist in your own town is a way to take a new route or to visit a new town. Play amateur photography, attend a local play, or watch the children playing at the park. These people have a great sense of humor!

9. Expand Your Awareness

Make the most of your free time by taking a class, learning to paint or trying something new. If you are feeling down, try listening to uplifting music or reading a book that interests you. You should find something you're interested in.

10. Remember Fun

Get a tear-off calendar, get a daily joke subscription, or find your sense of humor. A good belly laugh makes us feel better as fast as anything else.

MANAGE YOUR TIME

Planning and managing your time are important aspects of time management. Spending less time on some activities. Having a good pace increases an individual's efficiency, helps them accomplish more in a shorter period of time, reduces stress, and allows them to achieve career success.

BENEFITS OF TIME MANAGEMENT

Time management is one of the most important skills. Time management leads to better productivity and efficiency, less stress, and greater success in life. The following are some benefits of managing your time

The following benefits:

1. Stress relief

Making and following a task schedule reduces anxiety. As you check off items on your "to-do" list, you can see that you are making tangible progress. This helps you avoid feeling stressed out with worry about whether you're getting things done.

2. More time

Your daily life becomes more enjoyable when you manage your time well. The ability to effectively manage your time allows you to spend more time on hobbies and other pursuits.

3. More opportunities

Better time management leads to fewer time-wasting activities and more opportunities. Many employers look for candidates who are able to manage their time well. An organization's ability to prioritize work and schedule it is extremely valuable.

4. Ability to realize goals

Those who practice good time management achieve their goals and objectives in a shorter amount of time.

List of Tips for Effective Time Management

The following are ways to manage time effectively after looking at the benefits of time management:

1. Set goals correctly

Make sure your goals are attainable and measurable. SMART goals should be used when setting them. To summarize, aim for Specific, Measurable, Attainable, Relevant, and Timely goals.

2. Prioritize wisely

Prioritize tasks according to their importance and urgency.

Among your daily duties, determine which of the following are:

Do these tasks immediately. They are important and urgent.

Choosing the right time to accomplish these tasks is important, but not urgent.

If possible, delegate these tasks as urgent but not important.

Don't worry about them now: Set them aside for later.

3. Set a time limit to complete a task

When you set deadlines for completing tasks, you become more focused and efficient. You can also become more aware of potential problems if you decide on how much time each task needs before starting it. In that way, you will be able to take action.

As an example, suppose you need to prepare five reviews for a meeting. Yet you realize that in the time remaining before the meeting, you can only get four tasks completed. You can easily delegate these tasks to someone else if you become aware of this well in advance.

Despite this, you might not have realized your time problem until just an hour before the meeting if you hadn't bothered to check your tasks ahead of time. At that point, if you must delegate, then you may have difficulty finding someone to do the reviews, and they may have difficulty fitting the task into their day, too.

4. Take a break between tasks

Maintaining focus and motivation is difficult when performing many tasks without a break. Allow yourself time to relax and clear your mind between tasks. You might want to consider taking a quick nap, taking a stroll, or meditating.

5. Organize yourself

Make use of your calendar to better manage your time in the long run. Make a note of the deadlines for projects and for tasks that are part of the overall project. You may want to consider which days are best for specific tasks.

6. Remove non-essential tasks/activities

The importance of removing extra activities or tasks cannot be overstated. Make a list of what is important to you and what deserves your attention. It is better to focus your energies on the most important tasks and activities by eliminating non-essential ones.

7. Plan ahead

You should always start every day with a clear idea of what needs to be accomplished that day.

Whenever you end each workday, you should consider writing out your "to-do" list for the next day. The next morning, you can start right away.

Implications of Poor Time Management

Let's also consider the consequences of poor time management.

1. Poor workflow

If you fail to plan ahead and follow through on your goals, your efficiency will suffer. As an example, if it is crucial to complete several tasks together, a good plan is to complete them in sequence.

However, if you fail to plan ahead, you might end up spending a lot of time going back and forth. As a result, productivity and efficiency are reduced.

2. Wasted time

Wasted time occurs when time is not managed effectively.

Using social media to chat with friends while working on an assignment is a great way to waste time.

3. Loss of control

Having no idea what to do next makes you feel as if you've lost control over your life. As a result, you may feel more stressed and anxious.

4. Poor quality of work

When you don't manage your time well, the quality of your work suffers. For instance, rushing to complete a task at the last minute usually compromises quality.

5. Poor reputation

Clients and employers' expectations and perceptions of you are negatively impacted if you are unable to meet deadlines. It is likely that a client will take their business elsewhere if they cannot trust you to complete something on time.

MANAGE YOUR FEARS AND PHOBIAS

Whenever you run into situations or emotions you cannot avoid, do you allow yourself to be overcome by fear and anxiety? Learn how to overcome paralyzing behavior patterns with these expert tips

Fearful emotions are inherently unpleasant and we avoid them by nature. Do you want to plunge headlong into a potentially painful experience? In other words, by refusing to acknowledge the 'boogeyman' within, you become a victim. As a result, he typically hides from potential stressors and engages in endless distractions. However, you are also avoiding challenges that can lead to growth and joy. Furthermore, fear cannot be hidden forever. There will be a strike, Even though you try to suppress it. There's a high likelihood that it will strike at the end of your emotional stability.

In conceiving your fear-as opposed to shoving it into a distant compartment in your mind-you begin to lose the power it holds over your decisions.

Studies on Anxiety and Fear

The École Polytechnique Fédérale de Lausanne (EPFL) recently published a study in Science that describes how the brain must actually undergo a fear a second time before it is extinguished. Rodents were put into small boxes, then mild shocks were given and they were taken out. The scientists returned the mice to their boxes for a long time without administering shocks to them. In the beginning, the mice were frozen, but after repeated exposure to the box without any additional shocks, they eventually relaxed.

Humans may experience some relief from anxiety by repeating exposure to the trauma-causing event(s). Exposure therapy refers to the process of slowly and repeatedly exposing an individual to the fearful object in a controlled environment, as an example.

As an example, a person who is anxious about flying might begin by reading a story about a plane crash, and work their way up to going to an airport without boarding a plane, and then boarding a plane without taking off, and finally taking a short flight.

A person's anxiety level subsides with repeated exposure to the event (or events) that created the trauma in a safe environment, such as in a therapist's office.

Facing Your Fear

The suicide of her twin sister was one of the hardest traumas to treat for my patient, Doren. A fourteen-month-old girl who had been extremely close to Doreen's cousin fell to her death from a bridge fourteen months later. The mourning process was something Doren dreaded and feared. Grief overwhelmed her, and she feared that she would lose herself. She decided instead of coping with her emotions that she would travel non-stop to far-flung corners of the world. Though she felt lonely sometimes, she did not attempt to make friends for various reasons.

In the wake of an especially adventurous trip, she collapsed in my office. Sherry, I went on a hike near the Amazon and had Skype. It seemed hollow to spend time with a shaman. The experience made me want to share it with someone...with Beth."

The distress Doren was experiencing convinced her that it was time to stay home for a few months (her bank account would thank her!) and face her greatest fear: letting go.

Meetup, a social networking website, might be a good place for her to make new connections. Sometimes she registered for activities but her anxiety symptoms made it so intolerable that she stayed home at the last minute.

One time, I asked the question, "Why is it so frightening for you to let someone become close?"?"

After closing her eyes for a few minutes, she said, "If I let myself be vulnerable, it will kill me when they leave."

The person might leave for what reason do you presume?"

Beth and my sister left--everyone does."

You're still standing here, despite all of this. What could have been worse happened to you. Attending an event that involves pottery painting could be difficult, but how?"

The next day, she signed up for a hiking event with a group of friends. At our next session, she confessed that her anxiety symptoms had been so intense - sweating palms, trembling lips, palpitations- that she almost didn't make the hike. My intention was to remind myself that fear is a momentary emotion, as she says. *I will feel worse later if I run away from it.'"*

The group's next trip will be organized by her, since she had so much fun on the hike. Doren remembers, "I held my breath as soon as I got home and rescinded my offer after my anxiety became too much."

Doreen became a social butterfly soon after having been practically withdrawn for many years. Despite the anxiety, she had coping mechanisms that enabled her to control it and find relief from it. It still scares me to lose people, but it is even scarier to never find what I really desire—community."

Tips to Work Through Your Fear and Live Your Life

A therapist might be able to help you if you are experiencing overwhelming anxiety or fear, especially a phobia. In addition, the following suggestions helped some of my patients deal with being trapped by their fears:

1. **Allow yourself to sit with your fear for 2-3 minutes at a time.** Take a deep breath and tell yourself, "It's fine". Feeling lousy is like waves ebbing and flowing. When your sitting period is complete, do something nurturing immediately afterward: Call the friend waiting to hear from you; engage in an activity that is enjoyable and engrossing.
2. **Write down the things you are grateful for.** When you feel that you are in a bad place, look at the list. The list has been added.
3. **Remind yourself that your anxiety is a storehouse of wisdom.** Then send anxiety a letter saying, "Dear Anxiety, I no longer fear you.". Is there anything you could teach me?"
4. **Exercise.** Exercise can help you refocus (your brain can only concentrate on one thing at a time). Exercise

can be as simple as a 15-minute yoga video or as intense as an all-out workout at a boxing gym. You should consider the benefits of exercise, including a sense of accomplishment and a sense of grounding.

5. **Use humor to deflate your worst fears.** For example, what are some ridiculous scenarios that might occur if you accept an invitation to address a crowd of 500 people? *** I will be arrested for giving the worst speech ever *** I might pee in my pants at the podium in history *** In the audience, I will be heckled by my first boyfriend (girlfriend).

6. **Appreciate your courage.** During difficult times, Doren would tell herself, "Every time I do something that scares me even when I feel fearful, I am strengthening myself so that the next fear attack is less likely to stop me."

MANAGE YOUR FUTURE CHALLENGES

It is exciting to plan for the future, but it can also be extremely stressful. Your thoughts may turn to what you'll do after graduation as a college student. There are many paths that you can follow - work, school, a career, or even travel. You can handle the stress of planning for your future by solidifying your plan, avoiding comparisons with others, and concentrating on making graduation a positive event instead of a negative one.

Managing Anticipatory Stress

Make graduation a positive goal instead of a negative deadline. Graduation may become a dreaded date as a person prepares for the future. Nonetheless, you should congratulate yourself for making it this far and look forward to your graduation. Consider graduation as the start of a beautiful new era in your life.

Focus on your day-to-day experiences. When you start planning ahead, it's easy to become overwhelmed by thoughts of the future.

Taking time to appreciate your current situation is a worthwhile endeavor. Even though college can be stressful at times, you should find time to cherish the good moments you're having right now with your friends, family, and classmates.

It is common for people to look back on their college years as the best years of their lives. Don't worry about the future. Instead, focus on where you are right now.

Think positively about your future. You will only feel more stressed and down if you have a negative mindset. When you think of your future plans, try to keep a positive outlook. Consider all the things you might accomplish in the future as you consider your career path. Looking forward to the future should be an exciting prospect, not something to be dreaded.

Avoid comparing yourself to others. We are all on different life paths, and comparing ourselves to others ignores our unique backgrounds and struggles. Whenever you plan for your future, try not to compare your achievements to your peers, friends, or family members. You're probably stressing about the future with most of your friends as well.

Try not to get discouraged if you can't find a job right away. After college, you might find it difficult to find a job, especially if you're starting a career right away. Sometimes, people do not get the job they want when they first apply. If you're still young, the path you set for yourself may not be the one you go down. Stay flexible as you look for jobs.

Tip: During your college years, internships can help you plan for your future career. If you are in college, you should try to do an internship for at least one term to gain experience and figure out what career you would like to pursue after graduation.

Planning For Your Future

Evaluate your own skills and interests to decide what you want to do. As you get closer to graduation, you have probably acquired a good deal of skills through classes and internships. Your career path will be determined by combining your interests and your goals. If you want to pursue your preferred career path, you can go to graduate school, get a job, or start a business. Be sure to take your degree into consideration when planning your career path as well.

Reach out to your advisors to get advice. In addition to advising you on your class schedule, your advisors can also assist with career planning. Your advisor can offer you advice about achieving your goals if you ask specific questions about their career paths. If they have suggestions or tips that could assist you in the future, write them down.

- Possibly, you could ask, "Is there an online job board that I can use?"
- Does the field have a high demand for your services?"
- Is there anything you can tell me about getting a job at a large company?"

Go to graduate school if your job requires a higher degree. Undergraduate and graduate school are vastly different processes, and they usually require more time and effort to complete. Consider attending graduate school immediately if you are committed to pursuing a career that requires either a Master's or PhD. degree. You will probably not be able to apply for jobs with pre-med and pre-law degrees. If you work at your graduate program, you may be able to cover the costs of your graduate program.

Find a job if you're eager to work in your field or if you need the money. Look for a job that starts as soon as you graduate if you're excited about starting your career. Students are also concerned about student loans. When you graduate with a degree from an undergraduate program, you have about 6 months before you have to repay your student loans. Look for jobs to begin reducing your debt so you can get a jump start on the process.

- If you create a future budget for yourself, make sure to include student loan payments.

Visit your college's career center for job-hunting resources. Students are able to get advice and assistance from career centers at two- and four-year colleges. Make an appointment with yours and get advice about finding a job, writing a resume, and networking in your field.

You can also use a career center to match your skills and interests with jobs, if you aren't sure what career path you want to take.

Take a gap year to decide your path if you can. Think about taking between 10 and 12 months to figure out what you want to do after college. As you decide what to do with your life, you can work a minimum wage job, travel, or pursue a hobby. When deciding which direction to take, live with a family member to reduce your expenses.

FITNESS TIPS: STAY HEALTHY, MANAGE STRESS

Stress or anxiety can be reduced by practicing these methods:

Take a break. Get a massage, learn relaxation techniques, listen to music, or practice yoga. When you step back from a problem, you are able to get your head clear.

Maintain a healthy diet. You should not skip meals. Keeping a supply of healthy, energy-boosting snacks handy is a good idea.

Caffeine and alcohol trigger anxiety and panic attacks. Limit your alcohol consumption.

Sleep enough. The body requires more rest and sleep when stressed.

Get regular exercise to help you feel good and stay healthy.

The following fitness tips may be of interest to you.

Take a deep breath. Exhale slowly and inhale slowly.

Count slowly to 10. You may need to repeat this count up to 20 times.

Try your best. Be proud of your accomplishments instead of trying to reach perfection, which is impossible.

Don't try to control everything. Take the time to evaluate your stress: Do you really need it?

Humor is welcome. There's nothing better than a good laugh.

Be positive at all times. Embrace positive thoughts in place of negative thoughts.

Engage yourself. You can also become active in the community by volunteering or taking part in another form of community service, which gives you a break from everyday stress.

Learn what causes your anxiety. Would you like to talk about your work, your family, or your school? When you are stressed or anxious, keep a journal and explore the pattern you see.

Get in touch with someone. Let your family and friends know how they can help you when you feel overwhelmed. Consult a health care provider or therapist for professional assistance.

Exercise with moderate intensity (e.g. brisk walking) and vigorous intensity (such as running or swimming laps) will provide the most health benefits.

3 X 30: Jog, walk, bike, or dance for 30 minutes three to five times a week.

Do not stress about achieving perfect workouts, but rather strive for daily consistency. You should do 15-20 minutes of walking every day instead of waiting until the weekend to run a marathon. Frequency is important, according to a lot of scientific research.

Exercise should be fun or enjoyable. Class activities and group activities are often popular with extroverts. Individuals who are more introverted often prefer to work alone.

Get distracted listening to audiobooks, podcasts, or listening to music on your iPod or another portable player. Most people find it more enjoyable to exercise while listening to something they like.

You are more likely to stick to your exercise routine if you are accountable to a friend, partner, or colleague.

Whenever you start an exercise program, you need to be patient. It usually takes about four to eight weeks for sedentary people to feel coordinated and inadequate shape to feel comfortable exercising.

When you suffer from anxiety regularly, you don't need to rely only on medication for relief.

Here are some ways you can reduce stress and calm your mind:

Get up and move. The importance of exercise for physical and mental health cannot be overstated. You can feel less anxious and more relaxed by using it. During the week, work out for three to five minutes per session. Pick exercises that you'll enjoy so you'll look forward to them.

Sleep well. Sleep quality as well as quantity are both important for good health. Sleeping for eight hours each night is recommended by doctors. In the event that you are having difficulty falling asleep due to anxiety, try following these steps:

- Before hitting the hay, leave the screens behind.
- Follow a schedule as much as you can.
- Comfortable beds are essential.

Don't drink too much caffeine or alcohol. Anxiety can be exacerbated by both caffeine, which is an "upper," and alcohol, which is a "downer." Try to limit or avoid them as much as you can. It's important to remember that caffeine is found in foods other than coffee and soda. It can also appear in:

- Weight loss pills
- Medicines for headaches
- Yummy chocolate
- Drinking tea

Worry time should be scheduled. The idea of planning to worry may sound counter-intuitive, but doctors actually suggest picking a time to dwell on your fears. Consider how you can improve your situation by taking 30 minutes to figure out what bothers you. Set the same time for your daily "worry session.". Think about the things that make you anxious instead of what might happen.

Take a deep breath. Your brain receives a message that you're okay by doing this. Relaxing your body and mind is beneficial. Inhale slowly. You should be able to feel your belly rise slightly after eating. Keep it in your mouth for a second, and then slowly let it out.

Tricks for Coping With Stress

Stress can be managed in a number of ways. Some strategies and methods work for some people but not for others. "You should start with small, realistic adjustments, and don't expect perfection," Tribole says. The main thing is to find something that you like to do and that helps you feel centered.

Here are some other tricks for coping with stress:

Prioritize Self-Care

The last thing we think about when stressed is thinking about our own needs. Self-care should not be neglected by skipping meals or by ignoring other important aspects. Consider taking a step back and determining what you need. As Tribole suggests, think from the perspective of your pet: "What would you do for it?"Her reply is "I know.". Taking good care of our pets - feeding them on time and providing them with everything they need - is something we do for them all the time, so why not do it for us as well?

Delegate or Let Go

Stress is often accompanied by an extensive list of tasks we feel obligated to complete. Ask yourself, "Can that wait or can it be delegated?" When you are looking at your list, is it possible to wait?", Tribole says. Kellogg recommends you think about what you can do less of today instead of feeling overwhelmed by everything you have to do. There are so many things that we can cut back on that are nonessential and potentially stressful, whether it's mindless scrolling on Instagram or binge-watching Netflix at night.

Sleeping enough will help you feel full quicker and fit in your scheduled sweat session.

Get Enough Sleep

Getting enough quality sleep is the key to stress management. A lack of sleep can make us more stressed, and it also tends to raise our appetite for foods high in fat and sugar, says Dr. Janice Kiecolt-

Glaser, director of the Institute for Behavioral Medicine Research at The Ohio State University in Columbus. During sleep deprivation, the body is unable to regulate hunger in an appropriate manner. In fact, a study published in Journal of Sleep Research revealed that a single night of sleep deprivation could result in a significant increase in hunger hormone ghrelin. Similarly, a study published in Nature Communications in August 2013 found that sleep deprivation increases cravings for higher calorie foods because the primal brain is active during stress and helps keep the body alive. In addition, poor sleep makes you less likely to exercise, which means losing those benefits, including better moods and a greater level of resilience when stressed." Psychosomatic Medicine published a study that discovered that those with poor sleep were less likely to exercise. When patients with depression were treated with exercise, the results were similar to those who had antidepressants. Sleeping seven to eight hours per night is recommended for optimal health by the National Sleep Foundation.

Exercise Regularly

When we're stressed, fitness is usually the first thing to go. Exercise reduces stress and promotes sleep, so that's a shame. Several studies suggest that even one bout of moderately intense exercise helped people with chronic insomnia fall asleep quicker and stay asleep longer the day after they exercised. (Chronic insomnia occurs when someone cannot sleep at least three times per week for at least one month, while acute insomnia occurs infrequently.) These facts make exercise crucial during busy times. "Consistent moderate exercise has been shown to be helpful in managing stress and keeping stress hormones at bay," states Kellogg. Exercise reduces cortisol and adrenaline levels as well as releases endorphins, which are natural mood enhancers and painkillers. Naturally, this reduces stress.

Rather than thinking of exercise as something you add to your schedule, Kellogg recommends incorporating exercise into your daily routine. For example, when it comes to exercise, Tribole suggests going for a 10-minute walk, standing up or shifting positions every 60 to 90 minutes instead of worrying about fitting it in. Talk on the phone while standing rather than sitting," advises Tribole. Adding up small changes makes a big difference!"

Find Your Breath

Really! Shortness of breath and rapid heart rate are two common physiological symptoms of anxiety. The brain's autonomic nervous system can be controlled most effectively by breathing. Spend one-minute breathing deeply or listening to your breathing when you're stressed. Your body will be getting what it requires either way.

Stress eating can be prevented if we try to be present at this moment. Meditation can help with this!

Practice Mindfulness and Meditation

Meditation and mindfulness may seem like buzzwords, but they are actually ancient practices. There are entire training programs dedicated to the teaching of mindfulness tactics in order to cope with stress. Mindfulness-based stress reduction (MBSR) programs have been found to reduce emotional eating, but more research is needed to prove it.

Lean on Friends and Family

Having close personal relationships can really help," says Dr. Kiecolt-Glaser. But those close to us tend to isolate themselves and limit time with others when they're stressed - and that leads to emotional stress compounded by stress." A study published in Computers in Human Behavior in June 2017 showed that in-person support helped people cope better during stressful times - and text messages didn't. Having an awareness of the tendency to withdraw from others when stressed is the first step, but it can be difficult to break the pattern. Get the support you need from those around you by telling them you need it. Your doctor may be able to detect your stress earlier than you do, and take action before you know it's necessary.

Stress is something we all feel from time to time. It's normal. Nonetheless, we live our lives under excessive amounts of stress way too often. It's a bad thing. It affects us on an emotional, psychological, spiritual, relational, and physical level. If God is God, surely He can offer some wisdom to ease stress. Does He not care ... surely? Berni Dymet takes on stress in Stress Busters, a practical and powerful series of advice on reducing unnecessary stress and flourishing even under pressure.

www.ingramcontent.com/pod-product-compliance
Lightning Source LLC
Chambersburg PA
CBHW061648250726
48659CB00004B/1421